**Starting from Scratch**

By the same author:

WHITMAN'S OFF SEASON TRAVEL GUIDE TO EUROPE

# STARTING FROM SCRATCH

## A Guide to Indoor Gardening

# JOHN WHITMAN

**with the assistance of Mary Maguire**

Illustrations by Dave Brandon

**Quadrangle/ The New York Times Book Co.**

For information, address:
Quadrangle/The New York Times Book Co., Inc.,
10 East 53 Street, New York, New York 10022.
Manufactured in the United States of America.

Published simultaneously in Canada by
Fitzhenry & Whiteside, Ltd., Toronto.

Book design: Beth Tondreau

**Library of Congress Cataloging in Publication Data**

Whitman, John.
    Starting from scratch.

    1.  House plants.  2.  Plants propagation.
I.  Maguire, Mary, joint author.  II.  Title.
SB419.W293  1976      635.9′65      75-37371
ISBN 0-8129-0631-4

To Army and Randie
Art and Bobbie
Bill and Judy

# Contents

Introduction   xi

Chapter   I   *Plants for the Brown Thumb*   3

African violet   3
Arrowhead   12
Coleus   14
Common trees   19
Geranium   21
Jerusalem artichoke (Sunchoke)   26
Sansevieria   28
Spider plant   31
Swedish ivy   34
Sweet potato and yam   38
Wandering Jew   42

Chapter   II   *Plants for the Light-Green Thumb*   45
Common fruits   45
English ivy   49
Grape ivy   51
Herbs   54
Impatiens   57
Mango   60
Philodendron   64
Piggyback plant   66
Pineapple   69
Sugarcane   74
Taro   76
Wax begonia   78

**Chapter III**   *Plants for the Green Thumb*   **81**
Asparagus fern   81
Avocado   85
Caladium   90
Citrus fruits   93
Coffee tree   96
Dieffenbachia   101
Dracaena   107
Grape   111
Kumquat   114
Loquat   115
Macadamia   117
Papaya   120
Quince   122
Tamarind   123
Ti plant   125

**Chapter IV**   *Plants for the Deep-Green Thumb*   **128**
Banana   129
Coconut palm   133
Croton   135
Date palm   138
Ferns   141
Fig   149
Ginger   151
Guava   154
Kiwi fruit   156
Litchee   159
Monstera deliciosa   162
Passion fruit   165
Persimmon   166
Pomegranate   168
Prickly pear   171
Rex begonia   174
Schefflera   177
Sunflower   180

**Chapter  V**  *Secrets to Successful Indoor*   **182**
    *Gardening*
How to keep the costs down   182
The secret to successful potting   187
Starting from scratch with seeds   190
How to make cuttings root   195
When to water and when *not* to   198
How to overcome the conditions
  of a dry apartment   200
Basic tips on temperature   201
Ten basic rules on light   202
Rules of thumb for fertilizing   205
How to identify and avoid plant pests   206
Taking a vacation?   210

# Introduction

The cost of indoor plants is soaring, yet it is not necessary to spend a lot of money to have an apartment or house full of lovely plants. Both common and exotic plants can be grown from cuttings, pits, spores, runners, aerial roots, suckers, and seeds. By knowing where to get these and how to grow them, anyone can create a lush indoor garden very inexpensively.

Beautiful inexpensive plants can be found everywhere —for the asking. Ask a friend for a clipping from a coleus or for one of the "spiders" dangling from a hanging spider plant in its multicolored macramé holder. "And, by the way, couldn't I have just a tiny cutting of your philodendron plant?" The answer is almost always "yes."

Every day thousands of "potential" plants are thrown away. The overripe fruit at the local grocery store is invariably tossed into the garbage can. All that anyone has to do is to ask the produce manager to save those mushy papayas and puffy peaches. Most managers will gladly do this for one of their steady customers. It is possible to turn useless pits and seeds into lush avocado trees and date palms.

All that is needed to turn vegetal "odds and ends" into stunning plants you'd expect to find in a florist shop is step-by-step information on propagation, patience, and the time to care for your plants. Plant care can vary from occasional watering (for a cactus) to the TLC of a Luther Burbank, in the case of exotic plants—those that demand more than a passing glance and insist on constant weekly care.

*Starting from Scratch* gives step-by-step information on growing plants from practically "nothing" and includes hints which indoor gardeners will find invaluable if they plan to make their apartment more livable or to turn it into an exotic indoor jungle. The guide to indoor gardening answers two basic questions: What plants should I grow indoors? How do I go about it?

The guide answers these questions in four chapters by describing different kinds of plants ranging from those easiest to grow to those which are the most difficult to cultivate. The plants mentioned in the first chapter are for those people who think they may have a "brown or even black thumb" while the fourth chapter is devoted to plants such as bananas, coconuts, and litchees which will strain the imagination and know-how of budding Burbanks and Burpees, who have a "deep-green" touch.

A fifth chapter answers many of the basic questions which both the beginner and more advanced indoor gardener would be likely to ask. Also included are useful cost-cutting hints to show how easy and inexpensive it is to start a garden from scratch.

With prices rising, this approach makes sense. Furthermore, the experience of doing everything on your own adds a special touch and satisfaction to the art of indoor gardening.

# Starting from Scratch

# 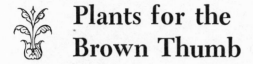 Plants for the Brown Thumb

You've probably tackled difficult plants in the past which were not suited to your apartment, office, or house. Certain plants can stand more abuse than others.

In this chapter you'll find some of the most pleasing and easy-to-grow plants. You can start them all from scratch with relatively little effort and at a low, low cost.

All it takes to change the color of your thumb to a light green is a little bit of patience, time, and detailed step-by-step information provided in this chapter.

As a novice indoor gardener, you should expect to make some mistakes. Even the most experienced growers lose some plants. In time you'll have all the plants mentioned in this chapter flourishing beautifully.

## AFRICAN VIOLET *(Saintpaulia ionantha)*

At the end of the nineteenth century a German baron discovered a lovely flowering plant in East Africa. Because it blossomed with violetlike flowers, the plant was named African violet. Its delicate blooms vary in color from wine red to light pink to blue. They lie in fluffy, fragile clusters above a rosette of deep-green leaves. The latter are covered with a light fuzz giving them a downy texture. Due to hybridization there is now an infinite

# AFRICAN VIOLET

**1**

Cut off a healthy leaf with a 2-inch stem.

**2**

The stem of the leaf should be placed ¾ inch deep in a Forsyth pot filled with perlite.

**3** **4**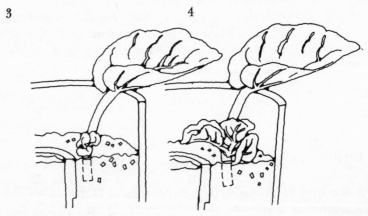

Within 6 to 8 weeks a small cluster of leaves should appear at the base of the leaf.

When the leaves of the young plant are ⅓ the size of the parent leaf, separate the two with a sharp knife or razor blade. Pot the young plant in an individual pot filled with sterilized soil.

variety of African violets available, some with flowers shaped like stars while others have curly, ruffled leaves. Added to the plant's immeasurable beauty is its pro- digious ability to reproduce—one reason it's a superb plant to start from scratch.

More indoor gardeners have started African violets from scratch than any other plant. The miraculous part about an African violet is that each of its leaves is a potential plant. Cut any healthy leaf from the parent plant, leaving 1 to 2 inches of stem. Make a clean cut with a sharp knife or razor blade. Here are some popular ways of propagating an attractive African violet plant from one leaf:

(1) Cover a glass or jar with tin foil, wax paper, or a plastic container top. The plastic top is the easiest to work with since it doesn't have to be kept in place with a rubber band. Poke a hole in the plastic top, place over the glass filled with warm water, and insert the stem of the leaf about ¼ inch deep in water. Keep this water level constant. Change the water twice a week until roots begin to form at the base of the stem. This should take from 2 to 4 weeks. When the roots are about ¼ to ½ inch long, plant the rooted leaves in a 2¼-inch pot filled with sterilized soil mixed with vermiculite or peat moss. Make sure the roots are planted as deeply and evenly as possible, but don't bury the stem any deeper than it was resting in the water. The leaf should be at least ¼ inch above the surface of the soil. Water the soil with warm water until it is thoroughly moist. Cover the pot with a large glass or inverted jar to keep the humidity high around the newly planted leaf. Lift this glass each day to allow fresh air to circulate and check on the damp- ness of the soil, which should never be allowed to dry out. The growing leaf should be placed in indirect light, not in direct sunlight. A small cluster of leaves will appear at the base of the leaf within 6 to 8 weeks. As

soon as they are one-third the size of the larger leaf, you can cut off the large leaf with a razor and start it again from scratch in a glass of water, as before. Healthy parent leaves can be used as many as three or four times to create new plants.

(2) An African violet leaf can also be rooted directly in perlite. Fill a portion of the jar with perlite and insert the leaf stem, which has been dusted with rooting hormone (*Rootone*), about 3/4 inch deep. Mist the perlite until it is thoroughly moist and cover the jar with wax paper, foil, or a plastic cup cover. The jar acts like a miniature greenhouse and should never be placed in direct sunlight. Open the jar each day to allow fresh air to circulate around the growing leaf. Check to make sure the medium is damp. A small cluster of leaves will appear at the base of the severed leaf within 10 to 12 weeks. At that time you should transplant the young African violet into an individual pot as previously outlined.

(3) Several African violet leaves can be rooted at the same time. Fill the bottom of a plastic breadbox with 2 inches of perlite. Insert the leaf stems, dusted with hormone, about 3/4 inch into the medium and mist thoroughly. Place the transparent cover over the box, and remove it once each day to give the growing leaves fresh air. Keep the soil moist at all times. Within 10 to 12 weeks you'll see small plantlets forming at the base of the leaves.

(4) One of the classic methods of rooting cuttings is in a Forsyth pot (see page 197). This is simply a large plastic pot or container filled with perlite, vermiculite, or sand, with a smaller clay pot placed directly in the center. Plug the hole in the tiny clay pot with cork, clay, or bubble gum, or cover the hole with strapping tape. By keeping

the small pot filled with water, the surrounding soil is kept uniformly moist as the water seeps through the clay. The leaves are placed in a circle around the pot with their stems, first dusted with *Rootone*, buried about 3/4 inch in the rooting medium. As long as the inner pot is filled with water, the moisture in the large pot will remain constant.

African violets can be grown from single leaves at any time of year. However, botanists suggest that the novice indoor gardener will be more successful in the spring-time, when there is better light and more warmth for growing plantlets. The end of March is a good time to take leaf cuttings.

Don't be discouraged if you lose some leaves in your first few attempts. African violets will sometimes wilt and rot. If this happens, pull up the rotted leaves and discard them. To increase the odds of getting an African violet on your first try, why not plant as many leaves as possible, using several different techniques?

Plantlets are usually ready for individual pots within 3 to 5 months; in another few months, the plant will begin to bloom. While this may sound like a long time, you'll be surprised how quickly it goes by and how fascinating the growth process is at each stage.

To start African violets from seed is a long growing procedure. Since the seed is so small, it must be planted in finely sifted soil. Don't cover the seed with peat moss or vermiculite. Instead, press it into the soil surface with slight pressure from a flat object such as a book. The seed requires warmth and high humidity. Mist the soil until it is thoroughly moist.

Cover the pot or flat with plastic or glass. Lift this cover each day to check on the dampness of the growing medium and to allow fresh air to circulate around the germinating seeds. Hopefully, tiny fleshy specks will begin to appear in about a month. Continue to keep the soil moist and warm. Place the flat in indirect light, but not in direct sunshine. At this point you should lift the cover about an eighth of an inch above the flat by sliding a thin piece of wood underneath it as a support. This will keep some humidity in the flat and will also allow air to circulate around the roots of the growing plants which will be about the size of a flat pencil point. As soon as the leaves are larger (thumbnail size) you can transplant them very carefully into 2½-inch pots. To do this use the tip of a pencil to uproot the seedlings. Try to take as much soil with the small root system as possible. Never bury the leaves in the sterilized soil of the new pot. Try to get the roots firmly imbedded in the soil. With warmth, moisture, and good indirect light, these tiny roots will fan out and secure the tiny plant to its new medium. For many growers this method is one of the most exciting ways to start African violets. It also has one wonderful advantage: packets of seeds often contain several different varieties of plants! You might have enough plants for all the plant lovers in your block.*

There are faster and surer methods, however, of starting this plant from scratch. Using multiple crowns and suckers is the key to overnight success in creating new plants.

A crown is the central portion of a plant from which new leaves originate. Small plants usually have one crown. However, as they mature, some African violets often develop more than one crown. Looking down at a plant, you might notice new leaves emerging in lovely rosettes in more than one place. Actually, there are two plants growing in the same pot. The development of a second plant from another is a wonderful gift of nature. You can take advantage of this by tapping the large plant from its pot. If the soil is slightly dry, you should be able to pull the two crowns or rosettes of leaves apart. Do this

---

* Very difficult—only for deep-green thumbs!

as gently as possible. Slowly, pull the intertwining roots of the two plants apart. You should end up with two clusters of leaves with a full root system dangling from each. Sometimes the rosettes do not pull apart easily, and you're forced to cut them apart with a sharp knife. If you have to cut crowns apart, gently dust the wound with a thin layer of rooting hormone (such as *Rootone* or *Hormidin*). Tap the crown gently with your forefinger so that any excess hormone drops off. A very light coating of hormone should stop root rot and encourage root growth from the wound. Plant the newly divided African violets in 3-inch pots. Mist the soil with warm water and continue to keep it *slightly* damp—almost on the dry side--to avoid rot where the stem was severed. Once the plants begin to show new growth, increase the watering so that the soil is moist, but never soggy.

Remember that using a sharp knife to separate the crowns may be risky. Some plants are lost this way. However, if two or more crowns separate naturally without wounds, you'll rarely lose a plant.

Don't be afraid to try this method since division of multiple crowns is the fastest way to get a new mature plant from an old one. Since many gardeners believe that African violets grow best as single crowns, it shouldn't be difficult to convince a friend to give you a divided plant.

How about asking a friend to save a sucker plant which shoots out from the sides of the parent plant? These suckers are tiny plantlets which sap the parent plant of its strength unless pinched off. Anyone who grows African violets has observed these and will be glad to give you one.

To obtain a sucker, sever it from the parent plant with a sharp razor, dust the wound with a thin coat of rooting hormone, and plant the potential African violet in a 3-inch pot filled with sterilized soil. Keep the soil slightly damp, but never soggy. In fact, the soil should be a little on the dry side to prevent root rot. As soon as the plant begins to show new growth, increase the watering so that the soil is always moist.

The African violet has a reputation for being quite temperamental. Yet, when given proper care and attention this hardy plant can withstand a wide variety of apartment conditions. Admittedly, the plant reacts poorly to dry air. But you can increase the humidity by placing the pot on a tray filled with pebbles and water. The bottom of the pot should not touch the water. Also, you can cluster a number of African violets together on one large tray to keep the humidity high. These plants look lovely in large groupings and lonely as single sentinels on top of a table or mantle.

Touch the soil around the plant each day to make sure it is moist. If the soil begins to dry out, give the plant a thorough soaking with warm water. Try not to spill water on the leaves as this can cause spotting. Don't mist African violets (misting is most efficient using warm water at environmental temperatures of 80°). If you want to remove dirt and grime from the leaves while the plant is in full flower, use a pipe cleaner or camel's-hair brush. Brush from the broad part of the leaf to the narrow tip. This is a tedious task, but the plant will benefit by the attention and care, allowing it to breathe more freely.

These plants can do quite well in a number of different locations. They prefer bright light without direct sun. An eastern or western exposure is excellent. A southern exposure is acceptable as long as the light is filtered through a thin curtain. Rotate the plant a quarter-turn each day to encourage uniform growth. Light promotes blooming while shade adds a deeper green color to the foliage. If your plant isn't blooming, try to give it more light. If you have very little available light in your apartment, why not try growing the plant under fluorescent lighting? Flourescent lights should be placed 12 inches above the plants and kept on for about 14 hours a day.

The ideal temperature for African violets is one which is comfortable for you as well—70°. Although the plant can withstand a drop of 10° at night, this isn't necessary as it is with other plants. Keep African violets out of cold drafts and away from freezing windows.

African violets grow well in light soil. You can obtain special mixes from a florist or add peat moss to sterilized potting soil. Many growers mix in a little charcoal. During its active growth, feed African violets at least twice a month using fertilizer at about one-half the recommended strength. It's better to use weak solutions of fertilizer more frequently than a heavy dose from time to time. Try not to get any of the fertilizer on the plant's leaves.

These plants also grow well in shallow pots. A 4- to 5-inch azalea pot is considered a good size for an average adult African violet. One of the advantages in keeping African violets in smaller pots is that they tend to produce more flowers when potbound.

Fortunately, African violets are rarely invaded by pests, but grooming is essential. Remove any dead blossoms and pluck off wilted leaves. A leaf will sometimes rot when it comes in contact with the sharp rim of a pot, especially a plastic one. If this happens, cover the rim with candle wax or tinfoil.

A final growing tip: African violets which are not growing well may respond beautifully to a change in scenery. Move a morose plant to a different window, place it on another mantle, put it above your kitchen sink—give it another chance!

In growing African violets you'll be experiencing a crash course in starting from scratch. The beauty, joy, and satisfaction that these plants have brought to millions are yours for the asking.

## ARROWHEAD, TRI-LEAF WONDER
### (Syngonium, Nephthytis)

The arrowhead is a tropical trailing plant with colorful foliage. It gets its name from the shield or arrowhead shape of its leaves. The stem of the arrowhead is often tinged with a light red color. When you break a stem, you'll often see a milky fluid exuded from the wound. Some indoor gardeners insist that this is a lovely "weed" to add to a plant collection.

The arrowhead prefers filtered light. An eastern or western exposure in most apartments is fine. If you don't have a great deal of sun, the arrowhead will grow well under fluorescent lights. Leave the light on for 12 to 16 hours a day, about 12 to 18 inches above the top of the plant. When you water the plant, give it a good soaking. Allow the soil surface to dry between waterings. Higher than average house temperatures encourage heavy growth, but the plant will thrive best in a range of 65° to 75°. During the summer feed the plant every 4 weeks. In the winter fertilize every 6 to 8 weeks. Misting will help keep the plant clean and free of pests, but you'll enjoy giving it a "shower" or foliage bath in warm water each week because the plant responds beautifully when kept humid and dust-free. A foliage bath consists of holding the pot upside down while swishing the plant's foliage in warm water. To stop the plant from falling into the water, support it between your middle finger and forefinger.

The arrowhead is an active grower and looks best if pinched back frequently, keeping it bushy and colorful. You can also root the portions or cuttings pinched from the plant.

A good cutting is one taken from the end of the stem where a new leaf is unfurling. Take a part of the stem which includes a leaf and an aerial root (a greenish-yellow bump on the reddish stem). With a sharp knife make a clean cut about ½ inch below the aerial root.

# ARROWHEAD

**1**

**2**

Cut off the end of a stem from which a new leaf is unfurling. Make a clean cut about ½ inch below an aerial root (a bump sticking out from the stem).

Place the cutting in an opaque jar or glass filled with water. Change the water as frequently as possible.

**3**

**4**

Roots will appear within several weeks. Allow them to grow 6 inches long.

Plant the cutting in a pot filled with sterilized soil. Try not to bury the stem any deeper than it was resting in water.

Place the cutting in water in an opaque jar with the aerial root just below the water surface. Change the water two or three times a week. Roots may appear as soon as 2 weeks or 3 or 4 weeks later. As soon as the cutting has a sturdy root system (about 6 to 8 inches long), pot the cutting in sterilized soil without burying the stem any deeper than it was when in water. You may prefer working with a Forsyth pot (see page 197).

This easy-to-care-for plant is quite attractive as a single cutting growing in a 5- to 7-inch standard pot, but it's even more attractive when several cuttings are planted in a 10-inch hanging basket. Placing many cuttings in the basket gives a fuller foliage effect, especially when the stems are allowed to hang freely.

If you have a friend with an arrowhead plant, why not ask for several cuttings? Since the plant grows best when pinched back frequently, it's a reasonable request. The ideal time to take cuttings is either in April or May when the plant is in full growth. The parent plant will respond beautifully by growing thick new foliage.

### COLEUS *(Coleus blumei)*

Colorful—that's the only way to describe a coleus, or painted-leaf plant. The lush, multicolored foliage of some coleus plants seems velvety to the touch. The ornamental plant, originally from Java, is a delightful one with its pink, rust, and purple spots blending into a fringe of pale or dark green on the leaves. It's an ideal indoor plant, which sometimes gets carried away with itself by growing so rapidly. The coleus's cheery color will catch your eye—whether in a friend's apartment,

# PINCHING BACK

## 1

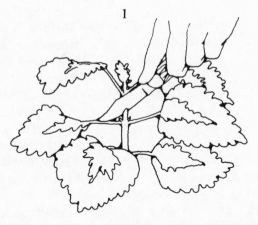

If you look closely at many plants, you'll notice tiny
bumps (nodes) just above pairs of leaves. With a sharp
knife, cut off the growing tip of the plant at this point.

## 2

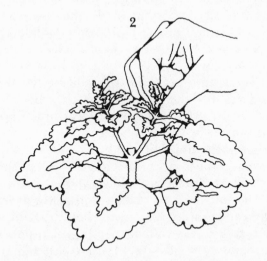

The tiny bumps grow into branches and in turn should
be pinched back. Pinching back encourages bushy growth
which is particularly desirable in such plants as coleus,
wandering Jew, impatiens, Swedish ivy, wax begonia,
avocado, and Jerusalem artichoke.

in a florist shop, or in your grocer's floral display in the early spring when the plant is less expensive.

It really isn't necessary to buy a coleus plant since a package of assorted seeds will provide enough plants for you and your friends.* The seeds can be purchased in many retail stores, or you can send for a package from George Park & Company, Greenwood, South Carolina 29647; Burpee, P.O. Box 6929, Philadelphia, Pennsylvania 19132; or Applewood Seed Company, Lakewood, Colorado 80215. The low cost of these seeds and the incredible variety of plants available make coleus ideal for starting from scratch. Try to get the "Carefree" variety of coleus which is colorful and bushy!

The seeds are miniscule, round, and black. Generally, they are enclosed in foil within the paper packet. Since they are so small try to scatter them over the surface of moist soil as evenly as possible. One way to do this is to tap the small foil container with your forefinger so that the tiny jolts knock the seeds onto the soil. If you hold the packet at just the right angle, only a few seeds will pop out of the packet at a time. Once all the seeds are scattered, cover them with a thin layer of finely shredded sphagnum peat. This should be no more than $\frac{1}{16}$ inch deep. Pat the peat down with a book or other small flat surface. Mist the soil and peat until thoroughly moist but not soggy. Cover the flat with a piece of glass or plastic to keep the humidity high. The ideal temperature for the seeds ranges from 60° to 65°. They should be placed away from direct sunlight.

Check the soil daily to make sure it isn't dry; misting will help keep it moist. The seeds should begin to sprout by 10 days to 2 weeks. When they begin to pop through the soil, remove the glass or plastic cover and place the flat in bright light. Continue misting the plants until

---

* Starting from scratch with seeds is recommended for growers with deep-green thumbs.

the plants have six leaves. Transplant the seedlings at this time into small pots. Ideally, coleus seeds should be planted in early March so that they are several inches high by late spring.

To get full, bushy plants pinch off the growing tip of 4- to 6-inch plants. A coleus will thrive on this kind of care and will become increasingly attractive with a "ruthless owner" who demands the most of his plants.

Too much sun can scorch the leaves of newly transplanted seedlings, but mature coleus plants thrive on bright sunshine and sparkle with vivid colors in a southern exposure with a minimum of 4 hours of direct sunlight. A coleus will thrive under fluorescent lights which should be kept on for at least 14 to 16 hours a day, about 10 to 12 inches above the plant. If a coleus ever looks dull and pale, it's lacking the proper amount of light.

A tough plant, the coleus will live in fairly dry apartments although it prefers high humidity. If you don't have a humid area, try to mist the plant as frequently as possible. Bring it into the bathroom when you're taking a shower. The moist vapor is beneficial as is bathing its foliage in tepid water. The ideal temperature for growing a coleus is 65° at night and 75° in the day. The plant will wilt if placed in a chilly area or if allowed to dry out. Keep the soil around the plant as moist as you can without making it soggy. Once watered and misted, the plant springs back to life after it has wilted. In the summer the plant needs lots of water, but in winter it can go for days without a drink until the soil begins to feel dry.

If you've planted coleus seeds in March, you'll have lovely plants by September. Once again, be ruthless and pinch off the top few inches of each stem covered with bright foliage. Pinch the stem back to a point just above two leaves. A quick pinch between your forefinger and thumb is all it takes. Don't throw away the part of the plant you've pinched off. Instead remove all but the top four or five leaves (somehow, it's so hard to throw away those gorgeous leaves) and place the stem in any moist rooting medium such as sand or vermiculite. Or do what many indoor gardeners do: place the plant in any water-filled container, such as a sangria bottle.

If you were astonished at how fast your coleus seeds grow, wait until you see how quickly the clippings sprout roots—just 3 or 4 days! Wait about a month before transplanting the cuttings into home-style pots (bean pots, for example). Settle the new plants into the rich soil with a good soaking. By February or March you'll have plants which in turn will yield enough foliage for a new crop of cuttings.

With some care and lots of attention given to it, your coleus will flower each spring. The cone-shaped tip of the main stem overflows with tiny, star-shaped, lavender blue flowers. These flowers tend to make a coleus look "weedy." You can pinch them off without harming the plant. Pinching back the coleus plant is probably the one secret to creating the kind of plant you'd likely see in a fine florist display. Also, keep the plant free of all dead leaves. Don't worry if a few leaves die occasionally, but don't let them rot on the plant. Watch out for mealy bugs, a kind of white fuzz which appears from time to time underneath leaves and at various joints. Take a Q-tip, soak it in alcohol, and touch the fuzz with the end. Wash the plant with warm water afterwards.

Since the coleus comes in so many different colors and can be trimmed in a variety of ways, it's one of the most versatile indoor plants. It can hang in a pot supported by a brightly colored macramé holder as with your other trailing plants. Or, pinched back, it is an ideal plant for bedside tables, the mantle over a fireplace, or the corner of your kitchen sink.

The coleus is the rabbit of the indoor plant world— it's a perfect plant for someone starting from scratch:

not only because it grows so rapidly but also because the extra clippings can be exchanged for new and more exotic potential plants.

## COMMON TREES *(Maple, Elm)*

In the spring, a most welcome sight is the stark sentinels of winter turning green. Soon the boughs are covered with a dense foliage. Only a few weeks after such trees as maple and elms emerge from this wintry lull they produce thousands of seeds—all potential plants for the inquisitive and offbeat indoor gardener.

The seed of the maple is one of the loveliest and most fascinating in nature. It looks like a light-tan wing of a dragonfly attached to a small round ball. These wings dangle in clusters from the branches of the tree until mature when they drop to the ground. The feathery wings of the seeds force them to spin like the rotary blades of helicopters. The small ball at the base of the seed always ends up facing downwards. Under ideal conditions this tiny ball takes root and eventually becomes a mature tree.

Each maple tree produces thousands of these feathery pods or seeds, any of which you can collect and grow into plants. This is also true of the elm but its seeds are smaller and more irregular in shape. A fuzzy edge surrounds the veined seed, indented at one end with a tiny, heart-shaped opening. These seeds are so light that they can be carried for miles by a strong wind.

Plant these seeds in a flat or pot filled with sterilized soil and cover with a thin layer of peat moss or vermiculite. As long as the soil is kept moist and warm, the seeds germinate quickly. Maple seeds can be placed about ½ inch into the soil. You don't have to point them downwards to get them to grow. Just lay them on their sides. The roots will naturally gravitate downwards. The smaller elm seed can be planted about ¼ inch deep. Both of these seeds germinate quickly, sometimes in only a few days.

To survive in the wild, seeds must grow quickly and be extremely adaptable. You should have no trouble getting these seeds to take root. As long as you keep the soil moist and give the seedlings bright light, they'll grow well. All seedlings should be planted in individual pots as soon as they have three or four leaves on the stem. During the winter they should be kept in a cool spot as soon as they've gone into dormancy. Gradually reduce watering in the fall. Keep the soil moist and cool (as low as 32°) in the winter.* In the spring increase watering, raise the temperature, and give the trees bright light once again. Fertilize the plants regularly in the active growing season and repot whenever necessary. It's best to repot in the spring just before the trees begin their seasonal growth.

You won't outdo Mother Nature at her own game, but you will find working with these seeds an enjoyable experience. They are a favorite with children as well.

* It's extremely difficult to "winter" plants in an apartment. If you have a friend with a garden, why not bury the pot there and let nature take over until spring? You can also remove the trees from the soil and place them in moist vermiculite or peat in a plastic bag where they can winter in a refrigerator. Open the plastic bag each week to make sure the peat is moist. The stem should be kept cool and moist at all times during this process.

## GERANIUM

This lush flowering herb was imported to Europe from Syria and South Africa in the early seventeenth century. Today, the façades of Swiss and German chalets are covered with window boxes filled to the brim with the brilliant blooms of these plants. The many varieties of geraniums can stagger one's imagination. Some are grown for their fanciful foliage, others sport leaves with the scent of nutmeg and roses, while others make ideal house plants and bear attractive flowers ranging in color from delicate salmon pink to brilliant red. Of all traditional indoor plants the geranium remains one of the most popular because it's easy to grow, easy to care for, and easy to love.

Although geraniums can be started from seed, the most practical way to start from scratch is with a cutting donated from a friend. Taking a cutting from a geranium plant is just as easy as snipping off a leggy stem of an ivy or coleus plant, but it should be much more precise.

With a sharp knife cut off 5 or 6 inches of new growth from one of the outer and sturdier stems of a healthy plant. New growth is light green compared to the tan woody growth at the base of the plant. Each cutting must have a growing tip from which leaves unfurl. A flower or flower bud may already be attached to the cutting. However, a cutting is better from a growing tip which has not yet produced a flower bud or bloom.

Buds appear from the center of newly developed leaves. If you look for the spot from which these leaves spring, you'll be looking at a branch or stem which can be cut and grown into a new plant.

Strip off all the large leaves except the two nearest the tip of the cutting. The leaves snap off easily if you push down on them with your finger. Also, remove the tiny shield-like leaves which appear on both sides of the node

# GERANIUM

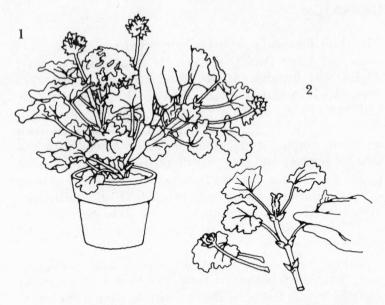

**1**

**2**

Cut off 5 inches of light green stem with a growing tip from which leaves unfurl.

If the cutting has a flower or flower bud, snap it off. Snap off all but the two leaves nearest the growing tip.

**3**

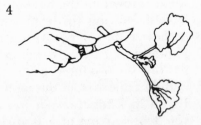

**4**

Remove all of the tiny shield-like leaves at the nodes.

With a sharp knife, cut through the stem 1/4 inch below a node which looks like a ring encircling the cutting.

5

6

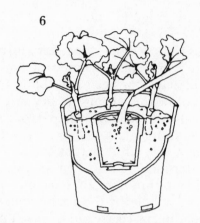

Dust the end of the cutting with rooting hormone such as *Rootone* or *Hormidin*. Tap the cutting gently against any hard surface to remove excess hormone.

Place the cutting in a Forsyth pot filled with sterile sand. Keep the cuttings in the Forsyth pot until they have roots at least 2 inches long.

where the larger leaves are attached to the plant's stem or branch. These tiny leaves will rot if planted in soil. Finally, remove any flower buds or flowers by pushing them in the opposite direction from which they are leaning. They'll break off easily with a slight push of your thumb.

The clipping you're preparing to root should be 6 inches in length with two large leaves at the top position of the stem. It should be pale green, somewhat fleshy, and covered with a light white fuzz. Wherever you've stripped off a leaf, you'll notice what looks like a ring around the cutting. Roots grow best from one of these rings.

With a sharp knife or razor cut about ¼ inch below any of these rings so that the cutting is approximately 4 inches long. Anything smaller than 3 or 4 inches is difficult to work with. Most healthy geraniums have many rings (or nodes) spaced at about ½ to ¾ inch apart so that you should be able to get a cutting of just the right length. A perfect cutting is stripped of all but two leaves, has no flower or flower bud on it, is 4 inches long, and has been cut about ¼ inch below a node.

Allow the cuttings to dry out for 5 or 6 hours to form a callus.* This will help avoid rotting. Cuttings can be placed in a glass of warm water which should be changed frequently until a root system has formed. However, a better method is to dust or cover the ends of each cutting with a thin film of hormone powder called *Rootone*. Poke a hole in the rooting medium (perlite, peat, vermiculite, or coarse sand) with a pencil  Place each cutting in a hole about an inch deep. The rooting flat should generally be 4 or 5 inches deep with several layers of crocking for perfect drainage. Water the soil until it is thoroughly moist. These plants will root beautifully in a Forsyth pot as well (see page 197).

A full root system will begin to form within 2 to 3 weeks as long as the soil is kept uniformly moist. Never let it dry out or become soggy since drenched soil will cause root rot as will high humidity. Don't cover geraniums with plastic or glass since they grow well in open and airy conditions.

When the roots are about 2 inches long, transplant the cuttings either into individual 3-inch pots or into one large pot which can support four or five cuttings. Keep the soil moist in all pots allowing it to go slightly dry in between thorough waterings. The plants should

---

* Some experts disagree with this and urge you to plant a geranium cutting immediately. I've had success with both methods. Also, many growers don't dust the ends of geranium cuttings with rooting hormone. They say this damages the cutting. I've been using hormone for years and have lost very few plants. Try both methods to find the one which suits you best.

adjust quickly to their new environment and sprout leaves within several weeks. If you see flower buds forming in the first 6 to 8 weeks, pinch these off. Spring cuttings will produce healthy blooming plants in the fall while cuttings taken in the fall will bloom in the spring. Wily indoor gardeners can have geraniums in full bloom throughout the year if they stagger their schedule of taking cuttings. Admittedly, poor light conditions make winter blooms relatively rare.

Geraniums are hardy plants and tolerate most temperatures although they prefer cool locations and adore bright light. Direct sunlight in a window may scorch them slightly in high summer temperatures, but in all other seasons a southern exposure is a superb location. Geraniums thrive on fresh air from late spring to early fall, but never let them get frost bitten. You should water the plants heavily whenever the soil begins to dry out. Geraniums prefer a dry spot, the kind of place you'd put cacti. Although they devour water in heat waves and appreciate an occasional bath, don't mist them since this can cause spotting and leaf rot.

Stems will become long and scraggly in high temperatures and poor light as the plant reaches for the sun. It's best to cut back long growth to keep the plant bushy and to encourage branching. The bottom leaves of geraniums turn yellow and drop off as the plant matures. Pluck them off to keep the plant attractive. This is a normal pattern for geraniums. This plant has a strong will to live and flower. Encourage blossoms by keeping the plant potbound and by giving it lots of tender loving care.

Geraniums look best displayed in large pots with several plants to a pot. Thick foliage crowned with numerous blossoms make this an ideal flowering plant for the indoor gardener. Since many people grow geraniums, you should have little trouble getting cuttings from which you can start new plants from scratch.

## JERUSALEM ARTICHOKE *(Sunchoke)*

The Jerusalem artichoke has nothing to do with Jerusalem and isn't even an artichoke, although it tastes similar to its namesake when boiled for 20 minutes, peeled, and sliced into small cubes which are soaked in butter. Despite its name, the Jerusalem artichoke is a native North American which was originally cultivated by Indians who cooked it in soup. Europeans heard about this food from Champlain who saw it growing in Cape Cod in the early seventeenth century.

You'll find Jerusalem artichokes in the gourmet section of the produce department in many grocery stores. They are generally available from October to June, although they're best in the late fall. These strange relatives to the sunflower are tightly bound in plastic covered packages with three or more artichokes in each. Look carefully at the tubers to make sure that they're clean. They should feel firm; soft spots indicate that the Jerusalem artichoke has spoiled.

In the case of the Jerusalem artichoke the indoor gardener either has to eat the artichoke or plant it. If you decide to forgo the eating enjoyment and wish to sprout these tubers instead, wash them in warm water. Place three or four artichokes in a triangle or square in a standard 10-inch pot, ¼ inch under the surface of sterilized soil. You'll get maximum growth if the artichokes rest on their sides rather than straight up and down.

Soak the soil with warm water and place the pot in indirect sunlight. Within 3 or 4 days you'll see pale-green sprouts poking through the moist surface of the soil. This plant grows so quickly that it appears as if someone has given it a shot of adrenaline.

The new plant will have a coarse stem covered with white fuzz. The leaves, which grow 8 inches long in full sunshine, will be smaller indoors but still sport the plant's characteristic white hairs. These are stiff on the upper surface of the leaf and softer underneath. Foliage tends to be light green and rather sparse.

Once the plant has at least 3 pairs of leaves you can cut the plants back just above a pair of leaves at the desired height to encourage bushier growth. The plant will branch into two wherever it's pinched back, but it will never be a beauty. Instead, it's the kind of plant which is more of a conversation piece than other conventional plants. Furthermore, it's instant greenery at a low, low price.

Taking care of a Jerusalem artichoke plant borders on benign neglect. Just water the plant when the soil gets dry and give it some light. You don't have to mist the plant at all. It thrives in both humid and arid apartments, can withstand extremes in temperatures, and will grow with any treatment.

Outdoors the Jerusalem artichoke grows 5 to 8 feet high and finally blooms with small disklike flowers which are sometimes yellow, or light purple. Commercially, the artichokes are harvested before the plant blooms when the roots are large and fleshy. You may notice that your plant loses leaves and dies down in the fall. If you want to keep the plant, store it in a cool, dark place until the spring. In late April or early May dig up the old tubers to see if new ones have developed by their sides. Plant these new roots just as you did the original tubers, and you'll be one of the few Americans recycling Jerusalem artichokes.

## SANSEVIERIA *(Snake plant, Mother-in-law tongue)*

Stark, dramatic, and almost ugly—this is a fair description of sansevieria with its stiff swordlike leaves. Here's a plant with an abstract appeal in its erect fleshy foliage, symbolic of its Indian and African heritage. These spears growing from sandy soil make superb house plants capable of withstanding all abuse with the exception of cold.

Also known as the "snake plant" and "mother-in-law tongue," sansevieria is the perfect plant for the impossible corner where no other plant has managed to survive. The plant, with its dark-green leaves, sometimes banded in yellow or gold, is a slow grower with few demands. Although it prefers high temperatures, it can withstand and grow in normal house conditions which include lack of humidity. It prefers actually to be dry. Good indirect light will spur it into active growth, but it also remains healthy in areas with low light. Water it heavily each time the soil drys out. Poke your finger into the pot to make sure the soil is dry underneath the surface. This plant can't stand soggy soil for any length of time.

Starting from scratch with sansevieria is a slow process unless a friend is willing to divide a large plant in two. To do this the plant must be taken out of the pot and a decision must be made as to whether the root system can be divided with a knife. A healthy root system will include tan carrotlike stolons supporting both the roots and leaves. Each one of these can be cut in two as long as they have a good root system and leaves attached. Sometimes in prying the roots apart, you'll discover that you already have one or two new plants, and it will not be necessary to use a scalpel at all. Plant the divided or cut plants in 5-inch pots filled with sandy soil. Soak the soil well and place the pot in direct light until the division shows signs of new growth.

A less dramatic way to start from scratch is to borrow

a leaf from a mature plant. Cut the leaf into 3- to 4-inch sections with a sharp razor blade or knife. Don't try to flatten the leaf if it's curled since you'll crack it. Dust the ends of each small section with *Rootone*—only the end which was closest to the base of the plant. Since it's very easy to confuse the top and bottom of new cuttings, always make an identifying mark on the cutting to show which end was closest to the root system of the parent plant.

Note that any cuttings taken from plants with golden stripes will not be identical to the parent plant. Cuttings will produce deep-green plants with no stripes. For those varieties, you can only obtain a "true type" plant by dividing a large plant as mentioned before.

The best time to take cuttings from a mature sansevieria is in the late spring. Place the newly cut sections about 1 inch deep in sandy soil that should be in a flat or pot 4 inches deep altogether. Or root the cuttings in a Forsyth pot (see page 197).

Soil around the cuttings should be kept slightly moist but never soggy. You can check on it frequently until plantlets begin to form at the base of the cutting. Continue to keep the soil moist with a mister. When two healthy leaves grow at the base of a cutting, transplant the cutting to a 3-inch clay pot. For the next 2 years new leaves and offshoots will form until the plant is ready for another pot.

Leaves grow to be about 10 inches high. Pot the mature plant in a 5-inch clay pot. The size of the pot will always seem small in comparison to the size of the plant. Sansevierias grow best in potbound conditions. Treat young plants as you would fully mature ones by allowing the soil to dry between watering. Naturally, these plants will grow best if given plenty of light.

Concerning plant care, sansevieria belongs in the brown-thumb section. However, when it comes to starting it from scratch, it's a challenging plant which demands

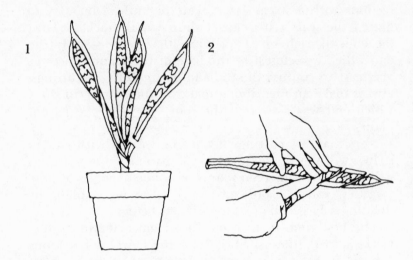

Cut a leaf from a mature plant.

Cut the leaf into 3-inch sections with a sharp knife. Try not to flatten the leaf or you'll crack it.

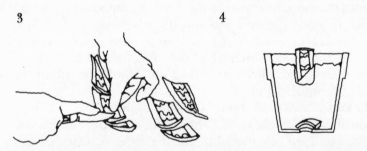

Cut off the top of each section so that only the bottom end is pointed.

Dust the pointed end of the cutting with rooting hormone before planting it in sterile sand.

5

6

A new plant will grow from the base of the cutting. When small leaves begin to unfurl, cut the plant from the cutting with a sharp knife.

Pot the young plant in a 3-inch pot filled with sandy soil.

a lot of patience. With proper care you'll have plants 2 to 4 feet tall, and occasionally they'll surprise you with greenish white fragrant blossoms in August. They open at night on leafless stalks.

## SPIDER PLANT *(Chlorophytum)*

A large spider plant does indeed look like a daddy-longlegs with its lovely green leaves arching upwards and out in a cascading effect. This is enhanced by wiry stems which bear tiny lilylike flowers, blossoming to tiny plantlets or "baby spiders." These add a delicate touch to the plant's great beauty.

The spider plant is one of the hardiest and easiest to grow of indoor plants. It can take plenty of abuse and mocks the brown thumb with its ability to overcome seemingly conscious carelessness. It's one of the few masochists in the plant world, but it laps up attention by growing vigorously and sporting rich green, pointed leaves, sometimes striped with creamy or yellow bands. It thrives on moist soil, although it can stand droughts due to water stored in its fleshy roots. The plant will grow in almost any light—north, east, or west. It will survive temperatures ranging from 55° to 75°. Furthermore, it's virtually pest-free and easy to start from scratch.

The tiny spiders which dangle from the mature plant are all potential plants. Spider plants are such prolific breeders that you'll often see five or six of these small spiders arching down from one plant. Each plantlet develops roots even while suspended in mid air. You can attach one of these plants to the soil in a pot by using a bobby pin or paper clip as an anchor. The little plant will soon grow a full root system and begin to grow rapidly. Once the plant is well rooted, snip it from the parent plant with a sharp knife and cut off the wiry stem.

A more convenient method is to reverse the process. Cut off the plantlet from the wiry stem and place it in a glass filled with tepid water.* Within a week or two it will begin to form white roots. If it already had a root system, this will develop more fully while suspended in the glass. Change the water every few days to keep it fresh. Once the roots are about 2 inches long, pot the small plant in a 4-inch pot. Water it thoroughly so that the soil settles around the delicate roots which will soon fill the pot with a maze of larger roots, white potatolike

* Spider plants react poorly to fluoride in the water. If you have fluoridated water, root cuttings in, and water mature plants with, distilled water. Spider plants also prefer soil without perlite in it, since perlite contains traces of fluoride. You can buy sterilized potting soil that contains no perlite at most florist shops.

# SPIDER PLANT

**1**

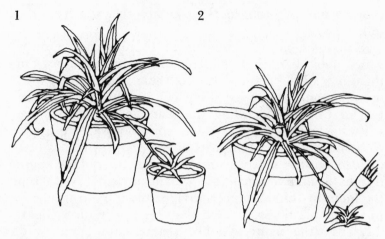

Plant a dangling spider in moist sterilized soil. Pin the plant down if necessary. Once the plantlet takes root, snip it from the parent plant.

**2**

If you prefer, cut the spider from the parent plant.

**3**

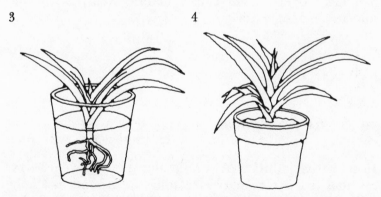

Place the spider in a glass filled with water. Change the water at least once a week. Always try to keep the water level constant until the spider has roots 2 inches long.

**4**

Plant the rooted cutting in a 4-inch pot filled with sterilized soil.

rootlets, and tiny root hairs which absorb water from the soil.

Sometimes, adult plants begin to form new crowns which look like tiny pointed spears jutting up from the center of the large plant. Let these develop fully over several months. You can then cut the mature plant in two or three by dividing the plant so that leaves are still attached to a root system. You may want to apply *Rootone* to the injured parts of the plant, which is best divided with a sharp knife. This surgery can be quite traumatic, and you may lose a plant or two. Try to keep the humidity high around a divided plant by wrapping it in a large plastic bag. Never place the bag in direct light. This way the plant will be in a miniature makeshift greenhouse, but will not be scorched.

Spider plants are so easy to grow from scratch that many people call them "friendship plants." You'll be giving tiny plantlets to many neighbors and friends. It's no wonder that this has been one of the most popular indoor plants for generations. It's a perfect plant for hanging baskets or an empty mantle from which the spiders can dangle freely.

## SWEDISH IVY *(Trailing coleus)*

In its native habitats (Australia and Africa) Swedish ivy cascades from trees or creeps along the ground as a soft rubbery pad of tangled trailers. Clinging to its fleshy stems which turn woody with age are dozens of light-green leaves with saw-toothed edges. They feel smooth and waxy to the touch and seem to shine in bright light. Sometimes, as you're passing this plant you'll smell a sweet, aromatic perfume. Everything about this plant suggests grace and tranquility.

The name of Swedish ivy, like so many common plant names, is a misnomer. The plant neither comes from Sweden nor is it an ivy. It's really a relative to the lovely and colorful coleus. As with the coleus, Swedish ivy is easy to grow from scratch. All you need to begin with are some cuttings from a friend.

These cuttings should come from the main part of the stem and are best if they are 3 to 4 inches long. Mature plants have woody stems at the base. Don't cut into these stems. Instead, slice off a fleshy growing tip which should be covered with shimmering leaves. Strip off all but three or four leaves left at the tip of the cutting or slip. Place the cuttings in a bottle, dark jar, or glass covered with aluminum foil. Only the green stem tinged with a light pink should be resting in the water with the leaves above the rim of the bottle.

You'll begin to notice root growth in as little as three days. Try to keep the water at room temperature and a little warmer as you change it every two or three days. When each plant has a bushy root system, it's time to pot the plants. You don't need a mass of tangled roots to be successful, and too large a cluster of roots at the base of the soft stem can be difficult to work with since these roots are fragile. Cuttings also take root very quickly if placed in a Forsyth pot filled with vermiculite (see page 197).

If you only have one cutting, pot it in a 4-inch pot. More than one cutting can be placed in a larger pot to simulate a more mature plant. Try to place the roots as deeply in the soil as possible without burying too much of the stem. The soil level should be just above the root system. Since these plants like to dry out between waterings once they're mature, a clay pot is better than a plastic one although Swedish ivy is durable and will grow well in either.

# SWEDISH IVY

**1**

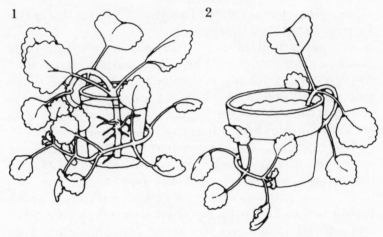

**2**

Take advantage of a single long cutting of Swedish ivy. Root a 10- to 14-inch cutting in water as you would a smaller one.

Once the cutting has a healthy root system about 4 inches long, plant it 1 inch from the side of a 10-inch pot.

**3**

**4**

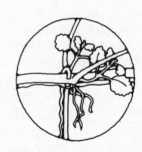

When new leaves begin to grow at the tip of the cutting, bend the plant around the inside of the pot, forming a circle with the fleshy stem.

Pin the plant to the soil wherever there is an eye or node (the spot from which leaves are growing). Roots will appear from the damaged stem while new growth will spring up filling the pot with foliage. Use this growing secret with coleus and wandering Jew as well.

Whenever you transplant a cutting from water into soil, soak the plants well in their new home and keep them out of direct sunlight. The soil should remain moist until new leaves begin to appear on the cuttings. This is a sign that they have taken and are beginning to grow normally. At this point you can begin to decrease the amount of water. Let the soil become slightly dry between waterings. Since your eyes can deceive you, feel the soil with your fingers. Poke your finger into the soil to see how dry it is under the surface. Whenever you water this plant, give it a good soaking until water trickles out the drainage hole. One good watering is better for most plants than three light ones.

If a friend gives you a long cutting measuring 10 to 14 inches, you can take advantage of this. Root the plant in water as you would do with a smaller cutting. Plant the long cutting about an inch from the side of a 10-inch pot. When the plant is growing well with new leaves emerging at the tip, bend the plant around the inside of the pot to form a circle with the fleshy stem. Pin the plant to the soil wherever there is an eye or node. Roots will appear wherever the plant has been damaged, and new growth will spring up filling the pot with light metallic-green foliage.

Swedish ivy is a fast-growing plant which appreciates indirect bright light. East and west windows are good. If the plant doesn't get enough light, it becomes leggy with few attractive leaves. Artificial light is excellent. Direct sunlight, as you'll often find in a southern exposure, generally bleaches the plant so that it becomes pale. Overwatering and misting in direct sunlight will cause spots on the leaves. The soil around Swedish ivy should be allowed to go slightly dry between heavy waterings. This plant can stand most house temperatures and even occasional chills, but it's not choosy about humidity. Since it does collect dust, it should be washed in tepid water every few weeks or given a sponge bath with a moist cloth. Wash the top surface of all leaves. But be sure to support them with your hand so that they won't snap off or crack!

Swedish ivy looks best in a hanging basket or in any place where it's allowed to grow freely as it hangs toward the floor from a mantle or high wooden table. The plant gets leggy if it isn't pruned. As with the coleus, ruthless pruning makes the plant more attractive with a full body of fresh foliage. Pinch off new growth which has a watery and somewhat soft stem—this is a potential plant for a friend. In three months your new Swedish ivy plant will supply enough small plants for every room in your apartment.

This charming foliage plant may even surprise you with rare whitish blue flowers in spring, if given the attention and care it deserves.

## SWEET POTATO AND YAM

Once regarded as an aphrodisiac in England, the sweet potato comes originally from the tropics and is a member of the morning glory family. The sweet potato, along with the coconut and gourd, took root in other lands after being carried by ocean currents, as accounted for by the European explorer Thor Heyerdahl.

Although the sweet potato and the yam are not the same plant, they are very similar in appearance and in growth patterns. A sweet potato will grow a lovely vine with attractive heart-shaped leaves. It can be trained to curl around a kitchen window or allowed to hang freely from an overhead basket. The vine is tough and will grow well in the light of an east or west window. The life span of each vine ranges from several months to nearly a year depending upon luck, care, and growing conditions. Once the vine dies, you can start all over again with a new potato. Here's how: most sweet potatoes and yams are treated with a growth inhibitor so that their "eyes" will not sprout on the grocer's shelf. This growth inhibitor makes it difficult for the indoor gardener to create a lush vine from a plump potato or young yam. If you have a small market or an organic food store specializing in fresh produce in your neighborhood, you can sometimes find fresh sweet potatoes that have never been treated with chemicals to prevent sprouting. You may even find some potatoes already sprouting new growth. Getting these potatoes to grow well will be easy.

Assuming there are no such markets or stores nearby, pick up some potatoes or yams from an ordinary food chain. Choose firm potatoes that don't seem soft or mushy to the touch. Wash the potatoes in warm water. You should not be discouraged if your yam says "no ma'am" and refuses to grow. Still, it's fun to try, and the possible plant springing from this tuber is worth the inexpensive gamble.

Armed with the conviction that your yam is going to grow, fill a jar with water, placing some charcoal in the bottle to keep the water from going stale. Stick toothpicks around the lower third of the potato which is quite stocky at that end. Three toothpicks placed evenly around the circumference of the potato will adequately support it when placed in the water-filled jar. The bottom of the potato should just touch the surface of the water. As the water evaporates, you'll have to add more so that the potato is in contact with water. Change the water twice weekly (daily if possible). Store the potato in a dark place until roots begin to appear and sprouts emerge from the plant. When this occurs, put the jar in direct light. As the small shoots grow and reach the height of 2 or 3 inches, you should remove all but

1

2

Choose a firm yam, preferably one with tiny purple specks growing from its eyes. Support it with three toothpicks so that it rests lightly in a glass filled with water. Put some charcoal in the bottom of the glass.

Place the yam in darkness until it sprouts roots and fleshy stems with small leaves. Change the water as often as possible to keep it from going stale. Always add charcoal.

3

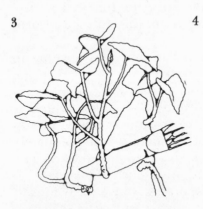

4

When the yam has many growing stems, cut off all but two or three. Make the cut at the base of the bumpy stem. Do not cut into the yam itself, which will continue to grow into a lovely plant.

Plant all the severed stems in a pot filled with sterilized soil. The tiny bumps at the base of each stem will sprout roots. Each of the stems will grow into a graceful vine.

two or three to encourage healthy growth in these stronger shoots.

Each of the tiny shoots cut from the parent plant can be potted. The bumps at the base of each shoot turn into roots which will support the growth of the stem and leaves above. You can easily plant a number of these shoots in one pot. Plant them as you would other cuttings, making sure that they never have a chance to dry out.

As for the parent plant, take care of it by adding 1 teaspoon of water-soluble fertilizer into the jar. Do this once a month, changing the water each time. You can also plant newly purchased sweet potatoes directly in soil without rooting them in water. Place them in a large pot filled with sterilized soil. Lay the potato on its side about 2 inches deep. Soak the soil with tepid water and keep the soil moist at all times. With lots of luck you'll have small sprouts poking through the surface of the soil within 2 to 3 weeks. If the potato begins to rot, dig it up and discard it. The chemicals aimed at stopping growth have succeeded too well.

Direct sun in an east or west window suits a growing plant well. You can train the vine to grow in whatever direction you choose by letting the tendrils follow small tacks or nails tapped into the woodwork or frame around a window. This attractive vine has been a favorite of indoor gardeners for many years. Unfortunately, modern methods of preserving the tubers make it more difficult to grow them now than it was in granny's time. But it's still a fun and enjoyable project, with a special appeal for children.

## WANDERING JEW *(Tradescantia, Zebrina)*

Both the *Zebrina* and *Tradescantia* species of wandering Jew are the royalty of hanging plants. Their watery soft stems are covered with 1- to 3-inch leaves varying in color from deep green lined with metallic silver to pink or yellow. The multicolored foliage is stunning when properly displayed in a hanging basket or on a mantle where the stems can hang freely to create a cascading effect of brilliant color.

Although native to Mexico and Brazil, the two varieties are hardy indoor plants and prolific breeders. The common name of wandering Jew is said to come from the plant's ability to take root on short notice, just as the Jewish people had to do for so many centuries. Its ability to root easily makes it one of the most popular house plants and an ideal first plant for the timid indoor gardener who believes she has a brown or black thumb.

All you need to start a wandering Jew from scratch is a cutting from an adult plant. Persuade a friend to clip off 4 or 5 inches from a full plant. Since these plants grow so quickly, you'll find that cuttings are there for the asking.

Cuttings root rapidly if planted in a Forsyth pot (see page 197). Or place the cuttings in a glass of water. Strip off the bottom leaves if they come in contact with the water. Cuttings grow best in dark jars or pots which don't allow light in. Darkness causes a concentration of plant hormones at the base of the cutting which leads to rapid root growth. Change the water three times a week to keep it fresh. Your cutting should begin to show signs of roots at the base of the stem within 7 to 10 days. If the stem begins to turn brown or looks like it's rotting, cut off the soft section and put what's left of the plant in a fresh glass of water. Generally, a cutting will have a healthy root system within 3 to 4 weeks.

If you just have one rooted cutting, plant it in sterilized

soil in a 4-inch pot. Try to place the roots as far into the soil as possible. Roots are quite fragile, but you still have to pack the soil around them so that the plant will stand up when watered. Give the plant a good soaking until the soil is thoroughly moist.

With a number of rooted cuttings, you can create a lovely large plant by potting all of the cuttings in one large pot. The size of the pot will depend on the number of cuttings, but remember that a wandering Jew grows fast and will fill a large pot quickly. Plant the cuttings evenly around the pot, about an inch from the edge. As in a smaller pot, the roots should be planted as deeply in the pot as possible. However, make sure you don't bury the stem of the plant any deeper than it was resting in water.

You can also grow a large plant from one long cutting taken from a mature wandering Jew. Cut off about 12 to 16 inches of one stem. Root it in water as indicated before. Plant the rooted cutting about an inch from the side of a large pot. As soon as you notice new growth on the plant with leaves unfurling at the end of the stem, curl the stem around the inside of the pot. The stem should look like a circle on the surface of the soil Wherever leaves are attached to the stem, pin it into the soil. Roots will soon form and new growth will create a full and bushy adult plant. This procedure takes longer than planting many cuttings in one pot, but it's the best way to take advantage of one long cutting when it's available (see page 36).

A wandering Jew plant grows and looks best in hanging baskets or pots placed in a spot where the stems can trail toward the floor. Most indoor gardeners would agree that you should pot these plants in plastic hanging pots with built in saucers which will catch water draining from the bottom of the pot. These plastic pots come in a variety of colors and are available in most retail florist shops.

This plant can grow so rapidly that it becomes spindly and ragged looking if you don't care for it properly. Like the coleus, it adores brutality. Pinch the stems back ruthlessly by removing several inches from the tip of the plant whenever it's growing well. If you have a number of shoots growing in one pot, pinch all of them back at the same time to keep the plant balanced in appearance. Pinching back the plant encourages bushy growth by increasing the total amount of colorful foliage.

Each one of the tips that are pinched off can be rooted in water. You can create new plants for yourself or give the cuttings to a friend, possibly in an exchange for a different indoor plant.

If you notice that hanging branches are beginning to rot where the soft stem touches the rim of the pot, cover the rim with candle wax. This should help the stems resist the sharp edge of the pot which can cause damage as the branches become heavy with the weight of thick foliage.

The wandering Jew appreciates a humid atmosphere which is usually lacking around hanging plants caught in mid air. You can supply this needed humidity by misting the plant frequently. You'll also discover that hanging plants are often thirsty. Although the wandering Jew can be allowed to dry out between waterings, it doesn't store water like cacti and succulents do. In fact, the wandering Jew is a heavy drinker, especially in the torrid heat of spring and summer. To promote colorful foliage, give the plant as much bright light as possible without scorching by direct light of a southern exposure. In most apartments the brightest light available is also the best. Don't be alarmed if your plant sheds leaves occasionally. Simply shake the pot and let these fall to the floor.

This colorful plant is virtually pest-free and carefree. One large wandering Jew plant can make a sterile hallway or stark apartment appear warm and livable.

# Chapter II

Plants for the
Light-Green Thumb

The jump from a brown thumb to a light-green thumb comes with more experience and a change in your attitude toward your plants. With confidence in yourself and affection for your plants, you'll probably have little trouble in getting the plants in this chapter to grow for you.

These plants are not easy to grow indoors, but they don't require the skill and constant attention of more exotic and unusual plants. Nevertheless, if you can get them to grow well in the "hostile" conditions of the average apartment or house, you're on your way to having a green thumb.

## COMMON FRUITS

Delicious fruits make a superb ending to any meal and a fascinating beginning to an unusual indoor garden. While most seeds and pits are tossed into the garbage, some can be saved to create a delightful group of small leafy trees that add a special touch to a barren corner.*

* All of the common fruits found in stores produce seeds which mature into trees that are useless outdoors. Furthermore, plants grown from fruit seeds last only one season in apartments or houses. They are a fun, short-term growing project, especially popular with children.

Although you may not witness apple or cherry blossoms you will add a hint of springtime to any room in your apartment.

Most people assume that all you have to do to grow an apple tree is to plant the tiny brown seeds in moist soil. Unfortunately, this isn't the case with any of the common fruits available on the grocer's shelf the year round. These fruits come from temperate climates where they drop to the ground and are chilled by cool fall and winter temperatures. In order to get seeds to sprout you'll have to fool them into believing that they've experienced a winter in the wild. Here's what you do with these popular fruits:

## Apple

Remove the shiny brown seeds from the core of a ripe and juicy apple. Rinse the seeds with water before placing them in a plastic bag partially filled with *moist, not wet*, peat moss,* vermiculite, or well-weathered sawdust.

Seal the bag and place it in the refrigerator. (The temperature should range from 35° to 45°.) Leave the seeds in the cool and moist environment for 60 to 90 days. Check once a week to make sure the peat moss is moist. Finally, you can take the seeds out of the sealed bag and plant them ¼ inch deep in sterilized soil. Plant about five seeds in a 5-inch pot and water them thoroughly. Pots should be kept in average room temperature of 68° to 72°. Don't let the soil dry out. As the seedlings arch through the soil with light-green stems, gradually move them into brighter light. When the seedlings have grown four additional leaves, transplant them to indi-

* You'll get moist peat moss if you soak it in warm water and then squeeze it to get rid of any excess water. Seeds should be placed in a damp but not soggy medium.

vidual pots. Since the process of chilling these seeds takes so long, you'll probably want to work with several dozen at a time to increase the odds of getting a young apple tree.

## Apricot

Most apricots now come from California, although they originated in China. The pits contain vitamin B-17, accepted in some countries as a potential control against the growth of cancer. The pit can be grown into a most attractive indoor plant with dark-green leaves shaped like a heart. Wash the pit well after removing it from the deep orange pulp and then follow the same procedure outlined for the apple. However, the moist, winterizing period has to last only 3 to 4 weeks. The ideal chilling temperature is 41°. Crack open the pit and plant the seed 1 inch deep in sterilized soil.

## Cherry

The smooth stones or pits of the delicious cherry can be grown successfully indoors. Follow the same procedure as for the apple. Cherry pits should be chilled for 120 days at the ideal temperature of 40°. As with the apple, chilling many pits will increase your chances of getting one to germinate at planting time. Chill at least twenty pits. Plant the pit 1 inch deep in sterilized soil.

## Peach

Scientists believe that peach and almond trees were identical at one time in botanical evolution. Pits from ripe peaches should be washed thoroughly in warm water before being given the "apple treatment" (moist, chilling temperature at 40° for 3 to 4 months). A number of pits should be chilled at the same time to insure germination. Crack the pit open and plant the seed ½ inch deep in sterilized soil.

## Pear

A favorite when fully ripe, the pear contains a number of small seeds in its core, like the core of an apple. Make sure that you find fully developed seeds which will be slightly larger than the apple's, dark brown and shiny in appearance. If the seeds are thin and shriveled, don't use them. Chill the seeds at a temperature of 32° to 40° for 2 to 3 months and plant them ½ inch deep.

## Plum

As with all the common fruits, the plum pit must be fooled with a moist, winter temperature of 36° to 40° for 3 months. As always, chill a number of pits just in case a few of them don't grow as expected. Plant the pits 1 inch deep in sterilized soil.

Now you know why seeds and pits didn't grow for you before. The secret is a little bit of abuse in a cool refrigerator. After this initial shock, treat the seeds with tender loving care, good light, warmth in spring, summer, and early fall, an occasional bath, and watering as the soil goes dry. That's all there is to the green touch with common fruits.

## ENGLISH IVY

The philodendron is the most popular house plant, but English ivy is a close second. Its popularity is well deserved, since it is an outstanding indoor plant—there are over seventy varieties to choose from. Some are deep green while others are flecked with white or yellow markings. The leaves can have the classic "ivy" look or can be nearly round in shape.

No matter what variety of English ivy you happen to choose, you'll discover that it's one of the most durable plants and can withstand a great deal of abuse. Although it prefers good indirect light, it can go for long stretches of time in darker areas.

As for watering, keep the soil moist but not soggy. If it does dry out for a few days, the plant will wither a bit, but it'll come back nicely after one good soaking with lukewarm water. English ivy prefers cool temperatures and can withstand dips as low as 35° at night. Don't deliberately test the plant by placing it in cold drafts, but don't be overly concerned about temperature as the plant is very hardy. Temperatures ranging from 55° at night to 70° in the day are perfect.

English ivy does like humidity, but it doesn't demand it. Resting the pot on a tray of pebbles is helpful, but it isn't necessary. You can mist the plant two or three times a week and give it a bath whenever the leaves get

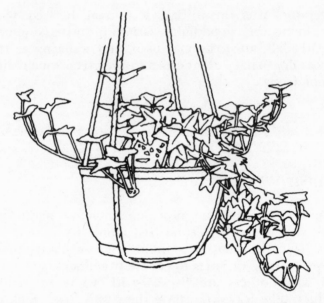

Cuttings are easy to obtain for English ivy, which should be cut back frequently for healthy growth.

dusty. Just swish the foliage in room-temperature water holding your hand over the plant and soil to stop it from falling out of the pot. English ivy adores frequent baths and will look better after this loving care. Never set a soaking plant in bright light. Allow it to dry out before exposing it to sunlight. Frequent warm baths also help prevent pests, particularly red spider mites, from invading the plant.

As for starting this plant from scratch, there's nothing to it. Simply ask a friend for a 4- to 6-inch cutting. Strip off the bottom leaves of the cutting and place the bare stem, with several leaves left at the tip, in a glass of warm water. No leaves should be touching the water. Add a bit of charcoal to the water to keep it from going stale and change the water twice weekly, keeping the level constant. Within several weeks roots will begin to form at the bottom of the cutting. Once the roots are 2 inches long, transplant the cutting into a 4-inch pot filled with rich sterilized soil. Make sure that all of the roots are planted as deeply as possible in the soil to encourage quick growth. The level of the cutting in the soil should be the same as the water level in the glass. Soak the plant with warm water and keep the soil moist. You'll know that the plant has successfully rooted as soon as new leaves begin developing at the end of the stem.

Rooting English ivy in water is fun since you'll be able to watch the plant's daily progress as the roots appear and spread out from the base of the stem. English ivy can be grown in water indefinitely if you don't want to plant it in soil. All you have to do is add nutrients to the water. Special fertilizers for water-growing plants are available in many florist shops. Simply tell the florist that you want to grow English ivy in water and have him suggest an appropriate fertilizer. Frankly, English ivy looks better potted than growing in water. It's a lovely trailing plant whose cascading stems can make a bare mantle into something appealing.

Rooting English ivy cuttings in water is not the most reliable method for getting new plants. You'll have greater success using the Forsyth pot (see page 197). Before planting the cuttings, dust the wounds with a light layer of rooting hormone to stimulate root growth. In several weeks you can check to see how the root system is developing. As soon as the roots are 3 inches long, transplant the cuttings to individual pots.

## GRAPE IVY *(Cissus rhombifolia)*

Although grape ivy is related to the grape with its long vine and clinging tendrils, it has no connection whatsoever with true ivies. Grape ivy and its cousin kangaroo ivy are terrific for indoor gardeners. They're hardy plants which can hang from baskets, be trained to curl around windows and doorways, or supported with a stake to mimic the trunk of a tropical tree covered with lush foliage.

Grape ivy originated in South America and the West Indies. This tropical plant has tannish leaves which become increasingly green with age. The pink undersides are covered with a light fuzz, in sharp contrast to the shiny upper surface which is almost glossy in bright light. As the vine grows, it appears as if silver buds at the end of the tendrils unfurl revealing fragile new leaves. The vines have a tendency to reach toward the sky before being weighted down by new growth which causes the growing plant to trail toward the floor.

Grape and kangaroo ivies demand little attention. They're not temperamental and will do well in the indirect bright light of an east or west window. There's no need to place them in the direct light of a southern exposure which is a prize spot to be reserved for more finicky plants. These pseudo-ivies adore moist soil but must not get waterlogged. Grape ivy thrives on high humidity, which you can supply with frequent mistings and warm foliage baths. Any normal house temperature will satisfy these accommodating vines.

Since grape and kangaroo ivies grow vigorously in spring and fall, most experienced gardeners pinch them back to encourage bushy growth which makes the plant far more attractive. Each part of the plant which is snipped off makes an ideal cutting with which to root a new plant.

Ask your friend to donate the cuttings to you. Cuttings can be any length, although the most manageable ones range from 6 to 8 inches. Remove all leaves from the stem except one set of three leaves at the end of the tip. Place the cuttings in a Forsyth pot (see page 197) or in an opaque jar with about 1 inch of the stem resting in

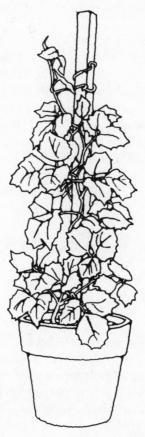

Grape ivy grows best when cut back. Planting cuttings in a Forsyth pot is the most reliable method for starting grape ivy from scratch.

water. Try to keep the level of water the same until the cutting begins to sprout roots. You should change the water twice weekly to keep it fresh. As soon as the cutting begins to form roots, let the rooting process continue until the roots are 2 to 4 inches long. Then plant the cutting in sterilized soil as deep in the soil as it was when rooting in water. The size of the cutting will determine what size pot to use. If you have several cuttings, try potting them all in one large pot to make a lovely basket of cascading trailers. Give newly planted cuttings a thorough soaking and treat them with the same care as adult plants. As long as you keep the plants misted and give them occasional baths, your plants should not attract any mealybugs, their biggest enemy.

Grape ivy is a gem of a plant—attractive, fast growing, and easy to care for. Even the most sophisticated indoor gardener will often have one in his collection. Don't let some of these cuttings escape your collection—get them from a friend.

## HERBS
(Chives, basil, parsley, rosemary, sage, sweet marjoram, thyme)

Herbs have long been associated with love, long life, and health. Their sensual fragrance and subtle taste make them favorites in any kitchen—a good reason why they're such exceptional gifts when potted or dried for friends. Although herbs are really outdoor plants, the skilled indoor gardener will soon have them growing among the plant collection with a bit of patience and know-how.

Starting from scratch with each of the seven most popular herbs begins with an inexpensive packet of seeds available in many florist shops and grocery stores. Of all, the three easiest to grow are chives, basil, and parsley. Although the other four are more difficult, they're worth the extra effort since they're long lasting and lovely.

You can plant seeds at any time of year, but the best time is usually in the spring since herbs will thrive as young plants in bright, warm sunlight. Plant the seeds in a seed flat filled with moist Redi-Earth or Fertilome soil mixes, ideally suited to tiny herb seeds. (There are 170,000 seeds in a 1-ounce packet of thyme.) Scatter the seeds as evenly as possible across the surface of the soil, then barely cover them with soil. Parsley seeds must be soaked in water for a full day before planting. Other seeds can be planted directly from the packet into the soil. Since there are so many seeds in each packet, you can plant just a part of the total and keep the remaining seeds, sealing them in an airtight jar at a temperature of 40° to 50°. Stored in this way, they'll be good for planting at a later date.

Mist the soil heavily after the initial planting, until it is thoroughly soaked. Keep the container sealed with either plastic or glass until the first seeds sprout. Be sure to lift the cover for 1 hour a day. Once the seeds have popped through the surface of the soil (generally in 2 to 3 weeks), place the flat in bright light. As soon as the seedlings are 2 or 3 inches tall, thin them out or transplant them to individual pots. Three or four seedlings fit nicely into a 5-inch pot.

Herbs demand lots of light and soil that is allowed to dry slightly between waterings. Provide parsley and chives with cool temperatures at night (about 50° in winter). All herbs thrive in the full sun of a south window. If lack of sunshine is a problem in your apartment, remember that herbs grow well under fluorescent lights. Keep them within 1 foot of the light, but don't let them touch the tube.

Very few pests are attracted to herbs. Nevertheless, don't take chances. Bathe the plants with tepid water every 2 or 3 weeks. Since you'll be eating the leaves of these plants, never use insecticides on them.

Never let herbs bloom since this will cause some of them to believe their life's work is over. Just pinch off any blossoms about to burst. This will redirect all of the plant's energy into creating lush new leaves full of scent and delicious oil. You can prune rosemary, sage, sweet marjoram, and thyme. All of the trimmings can be added to soups and stews, or whatever dish is on the menu. You'll find that fresh herbs outshine the dried variety—so much so that many people insist on using fresh herbs for all their culinary creations.

As you may know, you can often buy chives and parsley in local grocery stores. These plants are usually sold growing (or more likely dying) in tiny plastic pots or Styrofoam cups. Water the plants until the soil is thoroughly moist, then transplant them. They will need a new, larger home to survive. Pull the chives apart until you have a dozen or more plants from the original bunch. Don't be afraid of pulling carefully on the clump. With each chive plant you should get a long stringy root. Plant three or four of these small plants per 3-inch pot. From the original clump of chives you'll get seven or eight pots of properly planted herbs. Plant the parsley in a larger 4-inch pot where it has room to expand. Always eat the outer parsley leaves first since new growth appears in the center of the plant. Neither parsley nor chives should be dried. Admittedly, parsley is sold in dried form, but it's far better fresh.

All other herbs can be dried, although they lose much of their perfume and flavor in the process. You can use several methods for drying herbs. All begin with the initial step of cutting stems from the plants and washing them well in cool water. Spread the leafy stems on cloth and pat them dry. Now you have three choices. You can bake the stems in an oven at 200° with the door open until they're dry. You can put them in the bottom of a clean shopping bag hung in a warm closet until the leaves and stems are thoroughly dry (move them around from time to time). Or you can spread the stems over a screen placed on newspaper in a warm attic or closet until the stems are dry. The slower drying processes of the last two methods is preferred over the quick treatment in the oven, despite the longer time involved.

Once dried, shred the herb between your fingers. Discard any stems if you don't want them and place the herbs in tightly sealed jars which should be opaque (colored glass), or the herb colors will fade. And now you're ready for a Scarborough affair to which you can take your very own parsley, sage, rosemary, and thyme—either dried or in a pretty little pot.

## IMPATIENS *(Patience plant)*

Waxy and glowing flowers in an assortment of colors—pink, white, salmon, tangerine, and red—what more could an indoor gardener ask for? These free blooming gems shine on watery purplish pink stems and are among the easiest flowering plants to take care of. If you find this plant in an apartment of a friend, why not ask for several cuttings?

Cuttings from impatiens grow vigorously in water. Snip off a 3- to 4-inch tip of a fleshy stem and remove all but three or four leaves at the tip. Pluck off any flowers and flower buds so that the plant will direct all of its energy into growing a healthy root system. Within a few days, small roots will begin to form at the base of the cutting placed in a glass of water. Change the water frequently so that it won't go stale. Once a ball of roots has formed at the bottom of the cutting, plant it in rich potting soil.

Cuttings will also take root in perlite, vermiculite, or peat moss. A combination of these is also an ideal rooting medium. Follow the same steps as you would take for preparing a cutting to be set in water. Only this time, place the cutting about an inch deep in moist vermiculite. Make sure that all leaves are above the surface of the

Impatiens looks weedy unless pinched back. Take cuttings from the tip of the plant since they are rooted most successfully.

soil. A flat with 3 or 4 inches of rooting medium allows for the growth of a full root system, or use the Forsyth pot (see page 197). Check a cutting after 2 weeks to see if it has roots. You can do this with a flat stick like a tongue depressor or with your fingers. Simply scoop the rooting medium up underneath the plant and lift it just far enough to check for roots. If the plant hasn't rooted, carefully tamp it back in to the vermiculite. Once the plant has a good root system, transplant it to a rich soil either in an individual pot or grouped with other cuttings in a larger pot.

Impatiens can also be grown from seed which is sold in inexpensive packets at many florist shops.* The ad-

* Growing impatiens from seeds takes the skill of a deep-green thumb.

vantage of starting from seed is that most packets contain a wide variety of different flower colors—salmon pink to deep red. You may want to put the packet of seed in the refrigerator for several days before planting. The temperature should be about 40°. This is not necessary, but it will make the seeds sprout more quickly.

The impatiens seeds are miniscule and light brown in color. To spread them evenly over a moist growing medium of peat, vermiculite, or perlite takes a little practice. Open the packet and try to tap it gently at just the right angle so that the seeds will pop out sporadically instead of all at once on one small area of the soil. If all the seeds drop onto one tiny spot, you can correct the mistake by picking up the soil between your thumb and forefinger. Gently rub your two fingers together as you spread the soil mixed with the seed over the rest of the flat. Cover the seed with about 1/8 inch of soil and tap it down lightly with the flat surface of a book. Mist the soil until it's thoroughly moist, then cover the soil with a thin layer of finely ground sphagnum moss. Cover the flat or container with plastic or a piece of glass which will keep the humidity high. Be sure to take off the cover for 1/2 hour each day to allow fresh air in. Put the flat in a warm place until you notice light green seedlings poking through the surface of the soil. Even in warm and humid conditions, impatiens may take as long as 3 to 4 weeks to germinate. Make sure the soil is never allowed to dry out. If it does, mist it. The secret of getting seeds to grow is warmth and high humidity.

As soon as seedlings appear, take off the cover and move the flat to a sunny window. Direct sunlight in most seasons will not damage these plants, but be careful in the summer if you've placed them in a southern exposure. An overdose of sun can scorch tiny plants. The seedlings will soon grow a second pair of leaves. At this point you can transplant them either to individual pots or to a large pot in which you can grow a dozen or more plants. In transplanting, lift the plant gently by one of its leaves as you push up its roots with a pencil. *Never grab a seedling by the stem*—you can kill it!

The bright blooms of impatiens look best hanging from baskets in a semi-sunny location. It's better to hang them near a bright window with partial shade than in a hallway or dark corner. Keep the soil moist at all times. Impatiens adore cool nights with temperatures as low as 55°. Keep the humidity high for the health of the plant and to deter common garden pests, especially red spider mites. You'll find that in good light these attractive flowering plants grow quickly. Give them lots of room, but don't be afraid to pinch them back if they seem to be getting long and leggy.

All of the tips pinched off in pruning make good cuttings for other plants. Since these plants are loveliest in hanging baskets, you'll probably want to use a plastic hanger with a built-in drainage dish. These can be purchased in many florist shops. If you notice that the fleshy stems are rotting where they touch the rim of the pot, cover the rim with candle wax. Also, when taking cuttings from a friend, check for aphids—they adore impatiens, especially ones grown outdoors.

While impatiens are not quite as hardy as other foliage plants, they are still quite easy to start from scratch and are one of the most prolific bloomers in any indoor garden.


## MANGO

The apple Eve ate wasn't an apple at all—at least, that's what some scholars say. Instead, it was a mango, the "apple of the tropics."* From this delightful fruit you

---

* Others insist the apple was an apricot.

can grow a plant with intriguing foliage, related to both the sumac and the cashew tree. Although the princely Akbar had 100,000 of these trees planted near Delhi in the 1500s, you'll probably settle for one in your apartment.

You'll find mangoes in the produce section of many grocery stores from January through August. Most of these will be round and about the size of a large orange. Unripe mangoes are a dark green. As they ripen, the outer skin turns orange-yellow. Sometimes the skin will be speckled with tiny brown dots. Although this appears unattractive, it's really a sign that the fruit is ripe.

Mangoes are unpleasant to eat unless they're fully ripe. At maturity they have a juicy flesh somewhat similar to that of a peach. For this reason you can tell when a mango is ripe by giving it a gentle squeeze. It will feel soft compared to firm unripe fruit. The taste is rich and sweet, one of the reasons this fragrant fruit is so popular in the tropics. It's also packed with vitamins A and C.

Cut into the fruit lengthwise from either end. The blade of your knife will touch a hard pod inside the fruit as you do this. Separate all of the juicy meat from the pod which looks like the fuzzy wing of a large whitish-orange moth. This tough shell protects the seed inside.

You want to get to the seed without damaging it. Use a scissors or sharp knife to cut off the outer edge of the pod. Inside you'll see what looks like a large beige lima bean. It's covered with a wrinkled and somewhat worn coating. Soak this seed, without submerging it, in warm water for 5 days. Change the water each day so that it doesn't go stale.

At the end of five days the mango seed is ready to be planted. Strip it of its thin outer coating which will now peel off very easily. Plant the seed in sterilized soil in a 6-inch clay pot. The flat bean should be planted on its side about ½ inch under soil. Give it a good soaking with tepid water.

# MANGO

1

Slice a ripe mango lengthwise with a sharp knife.

2

Pry open the fuzzy pod inside with the tip of a knife or scissors.

3

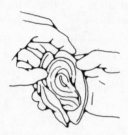

Pull the pod apart to get to the large lima bean-shaped seed inside.

4

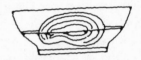

Soak the beige seed for 5 days in water. Part of the seed should always be exposed to the air.

5

Remove the thin skin from the seed after its initial soaking. Plant the seed about ½ inch deep in sterilized potting soil.

6

You can start the plant either in a small pot to be transplanted later or in a larger pot or tub which will be a more permanent home of several years.

While the seed is germinating, try to keep the temperature high and the soil moist at all times. Many seeds will sprout in 2 or 3 weeks although some take as long as 6 weeks or never sprout at all. For the indoor gardener it's a good idea to plant several seeds even though you may be satisfied with one plant. That's all you may end up with.

Once the mango has grown several inches high (the leaves are a wonderful shiny red at this stage), transplant it to a 10-inch pot or gallon plastic ice cream container. Redwood tubs and large wooden waste paper baskets make excellent containers for mangoes in later stages of growth. If you use a metal container, why not cover the inside with polyethylene to prevent rusting? Large containers should have several inches of crocking at the bottom for proper drainage. You should also punch or bore holes in the bottom of makeshift tubs so that excess water can run out. This will mean that the tub should be placed on a large clay or aluminum pan filled with marbles or rocks so that the bottom of the tub is never resting in water.

The mango likes plenty of sun, water, and warm temperature. In most ways you can treat it just like an avocado by misting its leaves and pinching it back to encourage branching and attractive growth. Although the mango is a splendid shade and ornamental tree in the tropics (where it grows as high as 70 to 90 feet), you'll find that apartment mangoes rarely outgrow their welcome. They also rarely produce the delightful pinkish white flowers that grow into mangoes, but the deep-green foliage with its shiny appearance makes this one of the most attractive exotic indoor plants. As long as you give it a warm welcome by keeping it out of cold drafts and away from frosty windows, it should become one of your favorite plants for many years.

## PHILODENDRON

In 1793 Captain William Bligh of *Bounty* fame introduced the philodendron to Great Britain on his return trip from the West Indies. Over 200 species of philodendron (meaning "tree-loving") grow wild in Central and South America. Philodendrons suit their name well since they are mostly climbers and vines. As young plants, many have solid leaves which begin to split as the plant matures. The philodendron makes an attractive foliage plant with its deep green, leathery leaves which vary in size and shape according to the variety of plant. All philodendrons are easy to grow and rarely attract indoor pests. Furthermore, they can be grown from scratch with very little effort—one reason they were particularly popular during the Depression.

One of the easiest ways to propagate many varieties of philodendron is to take a cutting from the tip of the plant.* Cut the stem just below a node where a leaf has grown. Try to include an aerial root which springs from the plant as it climbs up a support (see page 65). Cuttings vary in length from 4 to 12 inches. You can place the bottom of the cutting in water so that the bottom node and aerial root are submerged. Remove any leaves which come in contact with the water. Change the water frequently to prevent it from becoming stale. Charcoal should be added to the water to keep it fresh for a longer period of time. The cuttings can be placed in an east or west window where they should sprout roots in about 2 weeks. As soon as the roots are 6 to 8 inches long, transplant the cuttings into individual 4-inch pots filled with sterilized soil.

Many growers prefer to root cuttings directly in a sterilized growing medium such as perlite, peat, or ver-

* The ideal time to take cuttings from a philodendron is in April and May.

miculite. The best method for doing this is to use a Forsyth pot (see page 197).

You can grow a philodendron plant from seed, although it's quite difficult. The George W. Parks Seed Company, Greenwood, South Carolina 29646, stocks these seeds. The tiny black seeds should be planted about ¼ inch deep in sterilized soil lightened with peat, perlite, or vermiculite. Keep the soil moist by misting it whenever it starts to dry out. The seeds will germinate in temperatures ranging from 65° to 70°. Some seeds sprout within 2 weeks while others take up to a full year to germinate. As long as you keep the soil moist and warm, you'll have luck with these seeds. As soon as the seedlings have developed a healthy root system and are growing well, you can transplant them to individual pots. Growing philodendron from seed is a much longer process than starting plants from stem cuttings which are easily available from friends. After all, the philodendron is the most common household plant!

Taking care of a philodendron is not difficult since it's an adaptable plant. It needs little light to survive and has been known to tolerate 3 or 4 months without sunlight. Naturally, a plant will not be healthy or beautiful if kept in the dark, but it's a good plant for a corner with very little light.

The plant grows best with support such as a log imbedded in the pot. This is the way the plant is usually sold in florist shops. Plants grown in this manner have larger and healthier leaves, so try to give your philodendron, a true tree-lover, something to cling to. As the philodendron makes the climb upwards, it will send out small aerial roots to cling to the support. Philodendrons are not parasites drawing food from their host, but their aerial roots do absorb moisture and help the plant grow tall.

Philodendrons like loose soil with excellent drainage. Add some peat to sterilized soil to lighten it. Water the plant only after the top soil has been dry for 2 or 3 days. Let the water run down the supporting log so that the leaves and aerial roots get moist. Fertilize the plant once a month. Keep the leaves clean by misting them frequently. Gently wipe the top surface of the leaf when you sponge off any dust and grime. Whenever you clean a leaf, be sure to support the lower side of the leaf with one hand so that it won't break off. Philodendrons grow well in humid conditions. Since most apartments are dry, place the pot on a saucer filled with pebbles and water. The bottom of the pot should rest on the pebbles just above the surface of the water. If your philodendron begins to get too long and leggy, prune it back by cutting off the growing tips. Each one of the straggly tips can be used to make a new plant.

In tropical regions philodendrons become enormous plants with leaves up to several feet wide. Indoors, these monsters are tamed by the small size of pots they are planted in. Nevertheless, the foliage has an exotic appeal and manages to look good no matter how little care it receives.

## PIGGYBACK PLANT *(Tolmeia)*

This perennial herb grows wild in the rich carpet lining the damp forests of Oregon. It has become a popular house plant because it is tough, quite easy to grow, and unusual. The small 6- to 8-inch plant has hairy, heart-shaped leaves covered with white bristles. Often you'll find pale green baby plants clinging to the base of these mature leaves as if they are riding the parent plant piggyback.

Each one of these tiny plants can be grown from

scratch into mature plants. With a sharp knife or razor blade, cut off a leaf carrying one of the baby plants. Cut the leaf with at least 2 inches of stem. Insert the stem in moist sand or vermiculite and peg the leaf down with a hairpin at the base of the plantlet. From this small wound you'll see roots emerge within 10 to 14 days. To encourage quick growth, keep the sand moist at all times. Since piggyback plantlets adore high humidity, cover the pot with a clear plastic covering.

Another way of getting these plantlets to sprout roots is simply to peg one of them into the soil surrounding the adult plant. This way you won't have to separate the baby from its mother until a full root system has developed. This is really identical to the first method with the exception that there is never a separation of plants until the new plantlet is growing on its own. All that's needed is enough space in the original pot in which to peg down the leaf. Once the new plantlet has taken root, you can dig it up with a spoon, separate it from the parent plant with a sharp knife, and pot it in its own pot. Naturally, you can do this with any number of leaves to create an entire family of piggyback plants.

As with most other plants, you'll get an attractive foliage plant by placing several small plants in one large pot. Whether you're potting individual plants or a number of them, place the roots as deep into the soil as possible without burying any leaves. With a scissors you can cut away any of the old parent leaf from which the new plant has grown. Getting plantlets to grow is generally easiest in the spring.

Piggyback plants must be kept moist at all times. They react badly to droughts and often will die once they wilt. They thrive in good indirect light. East, west, and filtered south windows can provide adequate light for this hardy plant. Ideal temperatures vary between 55° and 65°. Since piggyback plants have fuzzy leaves, it's best not to mist them. Although they grow in humid conditions in

1

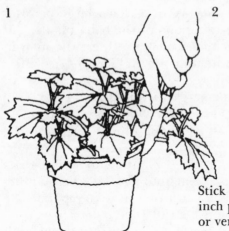

2

Cut off a leaf carrying one of the baby plants. Try to get 2 inches of stem with the cutting.

Stick the cutting into a 2½-inch pot filled with moist sand or vermiculite. Make sure that the base of the leaf is touching the sand. You may wish to pin the leaf to the sand.

3

4

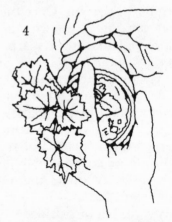

Roots will grow from the base of the leaf. Never allow the sand to dry out.

When you think the plant may have outgrown the small pot, remove it from the pot. If you notice that the soil has been filled with a compact mass of roots, transplant the plant to a larger pot (move up the size 1 inch at a time).

the wild, they'll survive in an apartment environment. You should give them a bath occasionally by swirling the foliage in lukewarm water. This will keep the leaves clean of dust and city grime. Sometimes these plants perish in areas plagued with high levels of air pollution. If this is a problem in your neighborhood, you may have less luck with this type of plant.

Other than that, piggyback plants are extremely hardy and in the same easy-to-care-for class as philodendrons and rubber trees. As long as you keep this plant moist, it will surprise you with its adaptability and charming appearance.

## PINEAPPLE

Although Charles V refused to eat a pineapple for fear of the strange fruit, it was a favorite among royalty for centuries and a fruit forbidden to commoners. Today, we commoners can enjoy this delicious and fragrant fruit at a reasonable price. It's still an aristocrat in taste. It also has a regal crown which can make a lovely indoor house plant that will become a conversation piece if properly grown.

Pineapples are easy to find in the produce section of a grocery store at any time of year. From the culinary point of view you'll want to choose a ripe fruit. There are several misconceptions about making this choice. Neither a leaf pulled easily from the top of a fruit nor a bright yellow color of the thick skin are necessarily signs of maturity. It is true that you don't want to choose a green pineapple which will never ripen properly, but the only way to tell whether a fruit is ripe is to give it a hard flick with your forefinger (pretend you're flicking a wasp off a friend's shoulder). A firm flick on the side of the fruit will result in a dull sound. The duller the sound, the more mature the fruit. The fruit should not sound hollow. As ridiculous as this may seem, it's the way Hawaiians choose ripe pineapples.

A perfect pineapple makes a dull sound, is heavy for its size (lots of juice), has a greenish yellow tinge, and supports no mold or leaking juice at its base. And, for the indoor plant grower that's not all. The perfect pineapple must also have a deep-green crown of vibrant leaves that have neither dried nor shriveled. A healthy crown will make a good potential plant.

When you cut the crown from the pineapple, take at least 2 inches of the core with it. The core of the fruit is the tough center section running from the crown to the base of the fruit. Most people don't eat it because it's hard to chew and not as juicy as the rest of the pineapple. So, you won't be giving up anything by leaving the core attached to the crown.

Scrape off any of the juicy flesh clinging to the core and let both the crown and the attached "dagger" dry out for two days. Pull off any wilted or yellowing leaves from the outside of the crown. This will help prevent root rot which is one of the main problems in getting a pineapple to grow. You can now place the crown in a 4- to 5-inch azalea pot filled with moist sterilized sand. Only the dried core should be under the sand. Place the plant in a shady area where it's warm and humid. Keep the sand moist without getting it soggy. Fill the cup in the center of the crown with water whenever it begins to dry out and mist the leaves once or twice a week. Within 5 to 6 weeks the plant should start to take root. It's tempting to check on the plant's progress during the first month or two by picking it up from the soil or digging around its base. Don't! As long as the plant is not rotting and seems to be surviving, leave it alone. Check for root growth only after 6 weeks. If the roots

1

2

Choose a pineapple with a healthy crown of vibrant green leaves. Without cutting all the way through the fruit, make an incision around the base of the crown.

Cut off the bottom of the fruit. This will reveal a tough central core.

3

4

Slice the pineapple so that the core remains attached to the crown of leaves. Let the crown dry out for two days.

Remove any dead leaves from the base of the crown before planting it in a 5-inch azalea pot filled with moist sterilized sand. Be sure to keep the cup in the center of the crown filled with water.

are growing at this time, move the plant into the same size pot with a richer soil (humus) mixed with ordinary, sterilized potting soil. This will be the plant's permanent home unless it outgrows the pot and needs to be transplanted.

Once your pineapple has begun to grow, place it in a bright location. Good indirect light is fine and can be augmented by fluorescent lights if necessary. Try to maintain a normal house temperature of 60° to 70° at the minimum. The root system should be kept moist without ever being allowed to become soggy. If you let the soil get slightly dry between thorough waterings, the pineapple will grow well. Keep the cup in the middle of the plant filled with water. The pineapple can absorb moisture through its leaves and will appreciate a full tank as well as frequent mistings. It also takes in nutrients the same way. Feed the plant with *very light* doses (one-quarter of the recommended dosage on the label) of commercial house plant fertilizer or fish emulsion, once a month in spring and summer. During the winter feed the plant once every 6 to 8 weeks. If you pour liquid fertilizer into the cup of the plant, don't allow the cup to dry out since fertilizer salts can burn the foliage. It's best to keep the cup filled with water anyway.

Warm temperatures and high humidity are the keys to success with pineapples. At all cost avoid cold drafts and any chance of frostbite. Pineapples are tough compared to many tropical plants, but they won't take the abuse of a chill from a Minnesota or Maine winter.

If your pineapple hasn't flowered after 2 years, give it a little push. How? The trick was discovered accidentally decades ago when a greenhouse burned down. To the amazement of the grower the pineapple plants in the greenhouse survived the fire and soon burst into bloom producing fruit. In the Canary Islands, greenhouses of pineapples are filled with smoke to encourage uniform flowering.

You don't have to burn your house down or even start a fire near your pineapple plant to get it to bloom. It's the ethylene gas in smoke which causes flowering, and this gas is also produced by rotting apples.

Enclose the entire pineapple plant, pot and all, in a plastic bag with an aging apple as a companion. Keep the bag tightly closed for five days before removing the apple and taking off the bag. A plant enclosed in a plastic bag should be kept out of direct sunlight. If the thought of dealing with an elderly apple is disagreeable, you can also induce flowering with a solution of 5 grams of calcium carbide dissolved in 1 quart of water.* Pour the solution into the cup in the center of the pineapple until it's full. Allow it to stay there for 24 hours. If any of the solution is still in the cup after a day, drain it out and rinse the plant with water. All you're doing is producing a different gas (acetylene) which has the same effect on pineapples as ethylene. Your pineapple should bloom within 4 to 8 weeks with this treatment. Try this only with mature and healthy plants. Tiny violet or blue flowers will blossom on a stalk shooting up from the center of the plant. About a hundred flowers appear on each stalk. Each one of them becomes a fruit so that a pineapple is really a hundred or more small fruits tucked neatly into the unusual object you pick up in a grocery store.

Since most grocery stores carry pineapples, this is an ideal plant to start from scratch. Not only do you end up with a delicious dessert, but you may also be rewarded with one of the most unusual indoor plants—all from a part of a fruit normally tossed into the garbage can.

* It can be difficult to find this carbide and can also be dangerous. Have an experienced grower help you with this.

## SUGARCANE

Cultivated in Asia since the fourth century B.C., sugar-cane is a perennial grass which grows to a height of 20 feet in both tropical and subtropical regions. The lovely green leaves, shaped like a narrow sword, fan out from a deep red stalk which is segmented in the same way as bamboo. The stalk can either be eaten raw or processed into sugar.

Although sugarcane is not a common item in most grocery stores, you will find it in some specialty shops as well as in a number of health food stores. You'll generally find it displayed with other exotic foods such as mangoes and papayas. The red stalks, often 5 to 6 inches long, are wrapped in plastic to keep them moist and fresh. Since you'll be starting from scratch with these pieces of cane, you'll probably want to buy several sections. The best sections are ones with bumps (nodes) already sprouting near the rings encircling the cane. Sometimes you'll have to ask the produce manager to order it for you. Cane is most commonly found in late fall—be sure to grab it while you can.

Growing sugarcane at home can be an intriguing adventure for the indoor gardener. If you have a long stalk of cane, divide it into six-inch sections with a sharp knife. Cut about an inch above or below the bamboo-like rings surrounding the cane to get these sections. Never cut into one of the rings since this is the spot from which the roots will grow. If you bought a small piece of cane, you shouldn't cut it at all.

Since the cane has a tendency to dry out, you should seal the ends of each section with wax. To do this you can drip hot wax onto a piece of cardboard and dip the ends of the cane in the waxy pool. The small sections of cane are now ready for planting. Always try to plant sugarcane as soon as possible after taking it from a store-

The secret to starting sugarcane from scratch is the choice of cane you make in the grocery store. Choose fresh cane with small bumps (the nodes) sticking out from rings. This will guarantee a high rate of success. Plant four or five sections of inexpensive cane in a large tub or 10-inch pot for the most attractive plant.

bought package. If it seems to have dried out, soak it in water for 24 hours to revive it.

You'll need a 10-inch pot for planting cane. Plant the sugarcane by laying it flat in sterilized soil about 3 to 4 inches deep. If there's a large bump on the piece of cane, have that facing upwards. This growing bump will begin to form small leaves within 4 or 5 weeks and a reddish growing tip will emerge through the soil. Soak the soil thoroughly and place the pot in the bright light of a south window for extra heat, but don't let the soil dry out. As long as the cane is kept moist and warm, it should germinate within several weeks. Individual sections of stalk planted in this way will sometimes sprout 6 to 8 new canes. These plants thrive in high humidity and like to be misted regularly at all stages of growth. Never mist the plant in direct sunlight!

Sugarcane grows quickly once it sprouts. In the wild it matures in 6 to 7 months while in most apartments it will grow more slowly. When the cane is several years old, you can cut it back and create new plants by slicing the stalk into small sections as you did before. The old cane plant which has been cut back often sends up new growth to replace the old.

As long as you have a bright window, lots of warmth, and the patience to quench this plant's thirst, you'll be able to create an exotic foliage plant from a tiny piece of cane.

## TARO *(Dasheen, Woo Doi)*

The taro is to the tropics what the potato is to the United States. Millions of people cook and eat this dark brown potatolike tuber as their staple food.* Although it is higher in nutritional value than the potato, taro is a specialty item found year-round only in a few specialty stores which carry unusual and exotic produce.

The taro has a thick, tough skin and weighs about 2 to 8 ounces. Like the potato, it has eyes and is extremely inexpensive. The flesh varies in color depending upon the variety and is toxic unless boiled. Once fed only to royalty in Hawaii, it's mashed into the famous *poi* of which some natives eat 10 to 20 pounds a day in tropical regions.

When choosing a taro root, be sure to buy one which is neither soft nor shriveled. The chances of getting a mushy root to grow are small. The plant which grows from the taro root has large heart-shaped leaves with reddish pink stems. In many ways it's a poor-man's caladium, but it does not have the caladium's rich colors. Instead, it supports 12- to 18-inch green leaves which have an exotic appeal.

The best time to plant this tuber or root is in late

* The taro root is poisonous until cooked.

April or early May. It needs lots of space in which to grow, so plant it in a 10-inch pot or in a large coffee can with drainage holes. Lay the tuber flat about 1 inch deep in sterilized soil. If possible, provide temperatures in the range of 75° to 85° to speed up germination. To get these high temperatures, you may have to place the can on a tin tray on top of a radiator. Heating cables are also very effective. Keep the soil moist after an initial soaking of the newly planted root.

The taro should begin to sprout within six to eight weeks. Give it bright light but not the direct sunshine of a south window. A west window with full exposure to the sun is a perfect spot for a sprouting taro. Keep the soil moist and place the pot on a dish filled with pebbles and water to raise the humidity around the plant. Never let the base of the pot rest in water or the roots of the plant will rot. You should have lovely leaves by the end of the summer under ideal conditions.

In the late fall, usually in November, the leaves will wither and die back. Don't be alarmed, as this is completely normal. Cut the foliage after it has yellowed and turned brown and give the plant a light watering. Don't water for 2 months afterwards. Store the pot in a cool (never cold) dark spot until early February. At that time water the soil until it's moist and keep it that way until new growth begins to appear. Sprouts generally emerge from the soil by early April.

Treat the new plant as you would a mature one by giving it bright light, a warm place, and plenty of moisture. Although taro is a hardy grower with unusual foliage, it is susceptible to frost. The plant's elephant ears make it a novelty with children.

## WAX BEGONIA *(Begonia semperflorens)*

With a name meaning "always flowering" how can you go wrong? The wax begonia has long been a favorite of both indoor and outdoor gardeners. Whether it's in a small pot in a sunny corner of an apartment or used as a border around outdoor plants, the wax begonia is outstanding. It's a small and bushy plant with polished leaves. Gathered above the shiny foliage are clusters of delightful flowers which range in color—red, pink, white, and salmon—and grow as single or double-bell blossoms.

Starting from scratch is easy with mature plants. Cut off about 6 inches from the tip of a growing stem and about ¼ inch below a leaf node. Pluck off any flower buds or flowers and place the cutting in moist sand, vermiculite, perlite, or peat. Pull off any leaves which come in contact with the growing medium. A 6-inch Forsyth pot filled with vermiculite (see page 197) makes the process of rooting cuttings much easier. Cuttings should take root in 4 to 6 weeks. If you prefer to start cuttings in a glass of water, submerge only the bottom half inch of the stem and change the water often.

As soon as the roots are 4 inches long, plant the cuttings in a 3- or 4-inch pot filled with sterilized soil. Never pot the plant deeper than it was resting in the water.

You can also start a wax begonia plant from seed which looks like reddish powder or dust. Plant it in a flat or pot filled with a mixture of pre-moistened peat, vermiculite, and sterilized soil. It's not easy to get the seeds to sprinkle evenly from the packet. Tap the open packet gently at an angle so that the seed is evenly distributed on the growing medium. Your hand should be about 3 to 4 inches above the soil. Use a mister to moisten the seeds. Cover the flat or pot with plastic or glass to keep the humidity high. The temperature should be between 65° and 70°. Open the plastic cover for a few

You can root cuttings from mature wax begonias, but it's more challenging to start these plants from seed.

minutes each day to allow air to circulate. Mist the surface whenever it begins to dry out. A gentle misting each day is advisable since seeds die quickly if they dry out. Seedlings generally begin to sprout in about 2 weeks. Take off the cover and move the plants into good light. The tiny leaves fan out and are barely visible, just tiny dots of green. When these plantlets have formed several leaves, you can transplant them to 2½-inch pots.*

Wax begonias will grow 6 to 18 inches high. Soil should be kept moist at all times. Poke your finger an inch into the soil and water if it's not moist at that level.

* Growing begonias from seed is very difficult and better suited to deep-green-thumb gardeners.

Maintain an even temperature between 60° and 70°. The wax begonia will live in light shade, but it prefers bright light. Since it has a shallow root system, you can keep the plant potbound which also encourages blooming. During active growth feed the plant with a weak solution of fertilizer once a month or more. Don't feed the plant while it's in heavy bloom. The wax begonia thrives on high humidity so you may want to place the pot on a tray filled with pebbles and water. The water should never touch the bottom of the pot or it will cause root rot. Finally, pinch the plant back ruthlessly to encourage bushiness. Each one of the cuttings when rooted will become a new begonia.

If you don't have bright light in your apartment, use fluorescent lights, which the plant responds to very well. Lights should be kept on for 14 to 16 hours a day placed about 8 inches from the plant.

The wax begonia is one of the easiest plants to start from scratch. It demands some attention but it's not temperamental. It's ideally suited to a person who wants a small, decorative indoor plant.

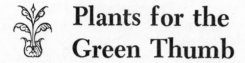

# Chapter III

# Plants for the Green Thumb

You should enjoy all of the plants mentioned in this section as you advance in your creative gardening endeavor. Once you observe that plants *do* respond to your loving care and attention, you'll realize you have the knack for getting things to grow. Yes, these plants require more than a passing glance and may even demand a weekly shower with you. However, anyone with a green thumb will consider this normal and enjoyable.

Information on starting each of these plants from scratch is detailed in a step-by-step procedure including helpful hints on its care.

## ASPARAGUS FERN

Several varieties of asparagus ferns are available at florists and enjoyed by house-plant gardeners. The bushy, slender *plumosus* species is often cut for greenery in floral decorations and bouquets. The *sprengeri* species has lacy, deep green fronds covered with inch-long waxy leaves that look like needles. This plant is ideal for hanging baskets or barren mantles as is the enthralling *meyeri* species. Because they don't produce spores, asparagus ferns are not really ferns at all. Instead, they produce berries, like their cousin the asparagus plant. Like asparagus they're tough and easy to care for. Small asparagus ferns are attractive, but the larger varieties are far more dramatic.

Florists often place four or five asparagus ferns in one large pot to create the effect of an enormous plant. The roots of these plants intertwine after several months and the fronds interlace so that it's almost impossible to tell the difference between this composed plant and each of its separate components.

If you or a friend has a large asparagus fern that seems to be outgrowing its pot, you can divide the plant into several separate ones. This is best done in March. Give the parent plant a good soaking several hours before dividing it. Gently knock the plant out of the pot and observe its heavy root system. The easiest way to divide an established asparagus fern into smaller plants is by cutting it into sections with a sharp knife. Be sure that each section has a root system attached to the fronds above. A large plant can generally be divided into two or three attractive plants. Give the divided plants a good soaking and keep the soil moist by frequent mistings. Division can be a traumatic experience for some plants. Yet, if it's done quickly and with a reasonable amount of skill, you'll have new and healthy plants with solid root systems. Division is an excellent way to keep a plant flourishing and fitting nicely in the scheme of your apartment. At the same time it gives you the opportunity to swap plants with a friend.

You may have a mature asparagus fern that you don't want to divide this spring despite requests from a friend. If you keep the plant intact until fall, you'll notice small fragrant flowers bursting into white blooms along the lacy fronds of this large plant. These flowers are followed by waxy-green berries which turn from light orange to deep red during the Christmas season. Large plants may produce several hundred berries, and it's not uncommon to find shriveled berries clinging to ferns as late as May.

Each of these berries can grow into an attractive indoor

plant. Pick the berries when they're ruby red, before they begin to shrivel and dry out. Squeeze each berry until it pops, revealing a small black seed inside. This can be a bit messy as the red juice squirts from the berry so you'll probably want to do this over a newspaper. Collectively, the black seeds look like fresh caviar. Let the seeds dry for several days after you've washed them thoroughly in tepid water to remove any pulp clinging to them. Properly washed seeds will not cling to paper as they dry and can be brushed off very easily when dry with a sweeping motion of the hand.

When the seeds have dried (after 2 or 3 days) they're ready for planting, although they can be stored for a few days if you want to wait. The seeds are extremely hard and have a thick shell. Since water does not penetrate this shell easily, you can help nature along by filing off part of the black seed coating with a nail file. Don't file on the end of the seed where you see what looks like a small white dot. Instead, file the seed in the middle on its sides. File just enough of the coat away to see a bit of white underneath, or until you see a tiny crack develop. You don't want to destroy the seed by filing too deeply. You can also use sandpaper to scratch off part of the hard shell. If you're concerned about damaging the seed, use a different method. Simply soak seeds in a glass of warm water for a full day.

Asparagus fern seeds can be planted first either in a pot or in a flat. Plant the seeds as far apart as space will allow. Although the plantlets prefer lots of breathing room, they can withstand some crowding since they're very sturdy. Cover the dark black seeds with no more than 1/8 inch of soil, or just about the thickness of the seed itself. Keep the soil moist with frequent mistings. By placing a piece of glass or some plastic over the pot or flat, you'll create an ideal miniature greenhouse in which the seeds thrive. Be sure to take off the cover for 1/2 hour each day to provide fresh air. Seeds of the asparagus fern "like it hot," so if you can keep the soil at 68° to 86°, you'll get faster germination than at lower temperatures.

Within 4 to 6 weeks you'll notice tiny green spears poking through the soil in search of light. At this time you should move the flat into the brightest light of your apartment. Also, be sure to take off the glass or plastic cover since glass magnifies the sun's rays which scorch the newly emerging plants. When the seedlings are 2 inches high, transplant them to small individual pots. When the ferns are 3 or 4 inches high, they'll begin to have the characteristic thin leaves of mature plants. It takes about a year for an asparagus fern to be full and attractive.

Asparagus ferns can also be started from cuttings taken from a mature plant. You should do this in either April or May. Cut off about 4 to 6 inches of the tip of a frond and place the cutting in sterilized soil, keeping it moist and warm at all times. Strip off any of the tiny leaves that come in contact with the soil. To keep the humidity high around the cutting, place a glass jar over it. Lift the jar for ½ hour each day to provide fresh air. Roots should begin to form within 2 to 3 weeks. As soon as a healthy root system has developed, you can remove the glass jar and treat the plant as you would other asparagus ferns.

Although the seeds of asparagus ferns grow best in a hot moist soil, the adult plants prefer cool temperatures varying from 60° to 72°. If the temperature goes higher than 72°, the plants survive but wilt a bit with dry, rather unattractive fronds. Temperatures lower than 50° will kill the plant. All varieties of asparagus ferns do well in almost any light, but they prefer an east or west window with moderate sunshine. Asparagus ferns thrive in a humid environment and adore frequent mistings and a weekly shower. Keep the soil moist, especially in spring and summer. In late fall and winter you can let the soil dry out between waterings. Overwatering will cause the leaves to drop. Asparagus ferns are as tough as they are attractive, but they do have one enemy: red spider mites that multiply in hot dry corners. You'll probably never see a red spider mite if you mist and wash your plants often. Asparagus ferns make lovely indoor plants. With tender loving care they grow healthier and more beautiful each year.

## AVOCADO *(Alligator pear)*

The avocado tree with a thick stem and waxy green leaves can be as beautiful as the most expensive plant you could choose in a florist shop. It all starts with the pit of the dark green fruit for sale in most grocery stores. While the fruit itself is delicious in salads and guacamole, the seemingly useless pit generally winds up in the garbage can.

With a little bit of patience that "worthless" pit can become one of your most prized house plants. While some indoor gardeners feel that the pits from avocados grown in Florida make better potential plants than pits taken from avocados grown in California or Hawaii, many experts disagree. They say that avocados have been bred to a point where the pits from any fruit—no matter what its origin—are just as likely to become lush adult plants.

If you'd like to grow an avocado tree, the directions are fairly simple. First of all, choose a ripe fruit. You do this by holding an avocado in your palm and gently squeezing it. If the avocado feels soft to the touch, then it's ripe. The darker green variety is firmer when it's ripe than the lighter kind.

When you cut the rough-skinned fruit in half, try not

# AVOCADO

**1**

Allow the pit from a ripe avocado to dry overnight. Remove the thin brown skin by peeling it off.

**2**

Cut off 1/16-inch slivers from the top and bottom of the pit. Soak it for 30 minutes in hot water (125° F) to prevent any chance of root rot.

**3**

**4**

Stick three toothpicks into the pit so that its bottom can rest in a glass filled with water. Be sure that the *fat end of the avocado* (the one with a small circular indentation in it) is submerged in the water.

When roots and a thin red stem sprout from the pit, pot it in a 6-inch pot filled with sterilized potting soil. At least one third of the pit should be above the soil surface.

**5**

**6**

To get the avocado to branch, pinch off the growing tip just above two leaves.

Another secret to successful branching is to cut straight down through the stem (about 1 inch) with a sharp knife so that the two leaves at the growing tip are split apart. Try to get half of the stem with each leaf. Do this only when the leaves are very small.

to slice into the pit. Gently pull the fruit in two and remove the brown pit which is imbedded in the fruit. The pit will be covered with about 40 calories of a greenish yellow paste—part of the oily avocado itself. Wash this off by gently rubbing the pit under tepid water until it is completely clean.

Let the pit rest overnight in a warm corner of the kitchen. During the night the dark skin will dry out, and you'll be able to peel it off in the morning. It peels off almost as easily as an onion skin, although it's slightly thicker. Underneath you'll see a light whitish tan pit with slight indentations. If you were to split the pit open, you'd notice a small toothlike growth in the bottom of the seed; this "tooth" will eventually become a plant. *Don't* split the pit open if you'd like to see it grow into an avocado tree.

Once the pit is isolated, take a sharp knife or razor blade and cut a thin sliver (no more than $\frac{1}{16}$ inch) from the top and the bottom of the pit. This is not difficult to do since the pit has about the same consistancy as the white part of a coconut. When you cut off these tiny portions of the pit, you'll probably notice that the color of the newly exposed flesh will turn a light orange—that's nothing to worry about. Cutting the avocado in this way helps the seed absorb water which in turn helps it to grow faster. To eliminate any chance of rotting, soak the seed in hot water (120°) for 30 minutes.

Now you can place the larger end of the pit directly into the soil of a 3-inch pot, leaving about one-third of the pit exposed to the air. Or you can stick three toothpicks into the pit about one-third of the way up from the larger end. Then suspend the avocado over a jar or paper cup filled with water so that the fat end of the pit rests comfortably in its warm bath. Just the base of the pit should lightly touch the surface of the water, leaving the rest to breathe and absorb sunlight.

The pit does not need direct sunlight, but it should be placed somewhere in a room where it receives indirect light. Since the pit can rot in stale water, it's a good idea to change the water every day. If you've placed a piece of charcoal in the cup, then it's not necessary to change the water as often.

The avocado should show signs of life within 3 months by sending up a sprout from the top of the pit and roots from the bottom. The roots often appear weeks before the tiny reddish sprout does. You may see this happen in as little time as 2 weeks if you're extremely lucky! Not all avocados grow, so it's wise to have three or four pits sitting in water at the same time in separate jars.*

Once the avocado sprouts roots and shows steady signs of growth, you can transplant it into a 5- to 6-inch pot. Be sure to leave a third of the pit above the ground so that it's exposed to light.

Avocados thrive in bright indirect light (filtered south or west window), in moist soil, and at high temperatures (85° is ideal but not necessary). When the young plant reaches the height of approximately 4 inches, you can safely cover the pit with fresh soil. At the same time you may want to pinch off the growing tip just above two leaves. Make an incision with a razor blade so that the thin stem is fully separated between the two leaves (see the illustration). This will force the avocado to branch, which makes a bushier and more attractive plant. You can follow this same procedure with each new branch to create two branches from one.

Avocados grow best in a spacious pot where the root system can develop. You can leave the plant in a 5- to 6-

---

* Recently, some avocados have been held in prolonged storage, which causes damage to the pit. If this trend continues, you'll have to try a number of pits to get them to root. Fortunately, indoor gardeners often come across pits that have not been damaged in this way.

inch standard pot for about 2 years or until the tree's roots begin to emerge through the bottom drainage hole. At that time it's best to transplant the tree to a larger pot. The hairless roots of the avocado are quite unusual compared to most roots of other house plants. They are also quite sensitive. Try to repot the plant without disturbing the ball of earth around the roots. If you moisten the soil several hours before transplanting, this procedure will be easier.

Anytime you plant an avocado—whether it's a sprouting pit or a bushy tree—use rich soil. Your avocados will appreciate this and grow accordingly. If the soil is rich, you can forget about fertilizing the plant for the first year. After the first year you can fertilize the tree every 4 weeks, usually in the spring and summer. By the fall and winter, cut down on fertilizing. At that time fertilize the plant once every 6 to 8 weeks. Liquid, water-soluble, and time-release fertilizers are the easiest to use.

Avocados like regular watering, but they drown easily. They also like being dusted and misted regularly—something which is particularly important in city apartments where soot and grime can gradually suffocate a plant. Another bit of information: in the tropics, windbreaks are built to protect the woody trees which snap easily. The avocado, unlike the reed, does not bend willingly.

It takes patience to grow an avocado, especially when you're trying to get the pit to sprout. Once the plant is rooted, though, it grows in quick spurts. If you can get the flourishing tree to flower, then you have a deep green thumb, hand, and forearm. Although a small branch can be covered with as many as 1000 blooms outdoors, it's very rare for avocados to bloom or produce fruit indoors. In any case, your love and care during the first 2 years will pay off in one of nature's finest ("from scratch") indoor plants.

## CALADIUM

When asked to associate a word with "leaf," 61 percent of the American public would respond with the word "green." The popular caladium is the wonderful exception to the rule. Here's one of the fanciest and most colorful foliage plants. The tropical plant, related to the lowly skunk cabbage, has several varieties, including ones with heart-shaped and elephant-ear leaves, which grow to be 8 inches long and 5 inches wide. Most indoor gardeners prefer the heart-shaped variety to the elephant eared. These thin, almost transparent leaves vary from light pink and deep red to speckled white. They are supported by fleshy pink, green, or mahogany stems. You can choose from an almost endless array of brilliant colors since over 2800 varieties of caladiums are available today.

Large retail florist shops stock the tubers from which caladiums are grown. Healthy tubers are solid to the touch—they shouldn't feel soft or mushy. They look like small dried-up rootlets with a number of buds or eyes similar to those found on a potato. Generally, healthy tubers are from 1 to 2 inches in diameter. Plant them anytime between February and April. The size of the tuber is a fairly good indication of how large the leaves of the plant will be.

To start from scratch you should plant the tubers horizontally about 2 inches deep in moist peat moss. Cover the pot or flat with plastic or a pane of glass to keep the humidity high. Take the cover off each day for a short time to allow fresh air to circulate freely. Never allow the peat moss to dry out. A gentle misting with warm water whenever the surface of the peat feels dry will keep the growing medium damp. Caladium tubers sprout in a temperature of 75° to 80°. Soil heating cables will be very helpful in maintaining the temperature.

Although there is no set time for sprouting, caladiums tend to send up shoots in a matter of weeks. As soon as you see growth breaking through the damp peat moss, remove the cover from the pot and move the growing caladiums into bright light. When the sprouts of the young plants reach the height of 2 inches, transplant them into individual 5- to 6-inch pots. If you would like a larger foliage plant, place three tubers in an 8-inch pot. Newly transplanted tubers should be planted at the same level (about 2 inches deep) in sterilized soil. Give them a good soaking and keep them out of direct light until the leaves begin to enlarge, showing that the root system is spreading throughout the pot.

Once the caladiums show signs of active growth, move them into a sunny east or west window or into a south window filtered by a thin curtain. Caladiums adore sunshine but will be scorched in a blazing sun. These plants need a lot of water, especially as the leaves become large. The larger the leaves, the more evaporation occurs. As long as the soil is always moist, the caladiums should thrive. High temperature and bright light are essential to get the most color from the brilliant foliage. During active growth you should feed caladiums twice a month with a commercial fertilizer *low* in nitrogen.

Caladiums will survive without high humidity, but they do prefer humid air. Setting the pot on a tray of pebbles partially filled with water will help keep the humidity high around the plant. Mist occasionally, and give the plant a foliage bath by swirling the leaves gently in warm water or by sponging them lightly with a damp cloth. Always support the leaves from underneath to avoid breaking or ripping.

In the late summer and early fall add fresh soil to the top of the pot, but be careful in scraping off the old surface soil since the roots are near the surface. Also, add some potash (potassium) to the soil to increase the tuber size. This late summer and early fall care is only important for indoor gardeners who want to revive caladiums after their dormant period.

The caladium will signal that it's going into dormancy by dropping its leaves, which either begin to fade or snap off. As this happens, gradually reduce and finally stop watering. Do not try to revive the plant. As soon as the leaves have died and the soil is dry, you can do one of two things: leave the tuber in the pot and store it in a cool place (55°) until early spring; or take the tuber out of the pot and brush off any dirt clinging to it. Place the dry tuber in a plastic bag filled with vermiculite and store it at a temperature of 60° to 65°.

After 4 or 5 months in its dormant state, the caladium is ready to be brought back to life. If the tuber has grown in size over the last year, you may be able to divide it with a sharp knife to increase the number of plants. Each piece of the root should have at least two eyes or buds from which shoots will grow. If you have taken the tuber from the pot, repot it just as you would the original store-bought variety. Soak the soil with warm water and always keep it moist. With luck, your caladiums will spring back to life in a warm and moist environment. Even skilled indoor gardeners with deep-green thumbs lose some of their caladium tubers during the dormant period. You may have to start from scratch again.

The caladium is one of the most exciting yet temperamental indoor plants. Its brilliant foliage is an outstanding feature. Because the tubers grow rapidly, it's possible to have a lovely plant within 2 months when starting from scratch.

## CITRUS FRUITS

Growing seeds of citrus fruits into striking indoor plants is a favorite pastime of thousands of gardeners. Grapefruit, orange, lemon, lime, and citron seeds taken from the fruit (commonly sold in the average grocery store) are all potential plants. Trees grown from these seeds grow slowly but have dark green foliage with a bright, shiny appearance. Sometimes the trees flower after many years, bearing heavenly clusters of fragrant white flowers. Anyone who has smelled an orange grove filled with blossoming trees will tell you that the scent is unforgettable.

Choosing fruit is an important first step. Try to choose the largest, freshest, and juiciest citrus fruit available. The seeds in dried-out fruit rarely germinate; and, naturally, you won't find any potential plants in the seedless varieties. If this is your first attempt at growing a tree from seed, why not start with a plump grapefruit? These seeds are among the easiest to start from scratch.

Remove the seeds from the juicy pulp and wash them in warm water. If you've chosen a large fruit, you'll find many seeds in it. The secret to getting citrus seeds to sprout is simple. *Never let these seeds dry out.* Unlike so many other seeds, citrus seeds should be planted immediately in sterilized soil. You can also soak them overnight in tepid water until you have the chance to plant them. The secret is to keep them moist!

The seeds should be planted about ½ to ¾ inch deep depending upon the size of the seed—the larger the seed, the deeper you plant it. Give the soil a good soaking. There are two different methods for getting these seeds to germinate.

*For spring, summer, and fall planting.* Place the pot in your refrigerator for 3 to 4 weeks. It should be in a plastic bag with several air holes. Check the pot once a week to make sure the soil is moist. Take the pot out after

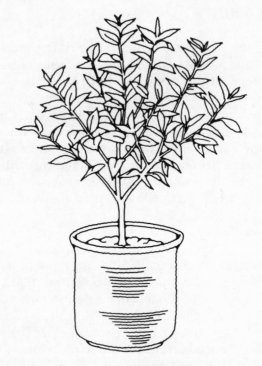

Instead of throwing away the seeds from a grapefruit, plant them immediately in rich soil. Citrus fruit plants grow slowly, so have patience—in time they will turn into stunning trees capable of living for decades.

this time. Keep the soil moist and warm until the seeds begin to sprout. When the seedlings are growing, mist them frequently and water the soil whenever it begins to dry out. Keep the plants in the brightest light possible.

*For winter planting.* Don't put the pot in the refrigerator. Instead, try to keep the soil temperature at about 80° to 85°. Soil heating cables make this very easy. The soil should always be moist. As soon as the seeds begin to sprout, move the pot into bright light and reduce the temperature to about 70°. Mist the growing seedlings often and water the soil whenever it begins to dry out. Transplant the seedlings as soon as they're 3 inches high (with four leaves) to individual pots.

Citrus trees demand bright light. If you can keep them in a window with a southern exposure, they'll grow best. From the time they're seedlings to the time they die decades later, these trees like to be misted frequently. You can give them showers occasionally to get rid of the dust and grime which accumulates in city apartments. Poke your finger into the soil to see whether it's moist and give it a good watering when the soil begins to dry out.

Although citrus fruits thrive in bright light, they do not need high temperatures. During the summer they prefer 60° to 75° with a drop of 10° at night (a plus for air conditioning). In the winter, temperatures ranging from 55° to 65° are good. You can cut down on the watering from October to February. Increase it again in early spring which is also the best time to repot plants that have outgrown their homes. Fertilize the plants once a month in active growing periods (from early spring to late fall) and less often in the winter. Use an acid house plant fertilizer for best results.

Pruning the plant will encourage branching and make the plant healthier. It is not necessary to prune citrus trees, but you can use the cuttings from the growing tips to create new trees. Cuttings should be about 4 inches long and include wood from the previous year's growth at the base. If there is a flower bud on the tip of the cutting, remove it along with the leaves at the base of the stem. Dust the wound where the wood was cut with rooting hormone. Tap the cutting on a hard surface so that any excess hormone is removed. Place the cutting about ¾ inch into moist sterilized sand and keep the temperature between 70° and 75°. Cuttings have the best chance of rooting if planted in late spring or early summer when they can also obtain warmth. For humidity you may wish to wrap the pot and cuttings in a plastic bag which should be opened daily to allow fresh air to circulate around the plants.

Never put this bag in direct sunlight! Cuttings normally begin to form roots within 6 to 12 weeks. They can be potted in individual 4-inch pots where they should grow well for a year. After that transplant them into larger pots as they increase in size.

Citrus fruit plants will provide you with lovely indoor foliage provided you give them the bright light they demand year round. Some plants will live indoors for as long as 25 years.

## COFFEE TREE

Have you ever seen a coffee plant for sale or in a friend's apartment? Probably not, since florist shops rarely stock these exotic plants.

Most coffee trees are grown in Brazil and Colombia, although they're actually native to Africa (Madagascar). The coffee tree (an evergreen) grows best in semi-tropical climates. The tree matures in about 5 to 7 years when it bears delicate white, star-shaped flowers with a fragrance similar to that of orange blossoms—one of the most lovely scents imaginable. It usually blooms in July. From the pollinated flowers emerge deep red berries which could easily be mistaken for cherries. Each of these berries yields two beans which have an oval shape—one side of each bean being flatter than the other.

The two seeds or beans in every berry are surrounded by a rich, pulpy substance. When the skin and pulp are removed, the seeds are exposed, which are then roasted and ground.

Coffee seeds found in most stores have been roasted and won't germinate. You'll have to order seeds from a seed company.

Most coffee trees are initially grown from coffee beans or seeds—whether in Brazil or in a New York apartment. From the point of view of the indoor gardener the delicious coffee beans found on your grocer's shelf are useless. Since they've been roasted, they'll never germinate. However, a few health food stores and many seed houses across the country stock live, unroasted coffee beans.* A packet of 10 to 12 seeds costs approximately one dollar. John Brudy's Rare Plant House, POB 1348, Cocoa Beach,

* It's possible to get seeds from health food stores to germinate, but it's very difficult and risky. Coffee seeds lose potency if not properly stored.

Florida 32931, generally has seeds in stock, especially in March and April. So does J. L. Hudson, Seedsman, P.O. Box 1058, Redwood City, California 94064.

To get the beans or seeds to germinate, soak them overnight in a glass of warm water. Then, place them ½ inch deep in the soil of a baking pan, flat, or bottom portion of a milk container with good drainage (home-made flats must have small holes through which excess water can drain). Put a seed in each corner about an inch from the side of the container. Coffee plants don't like to be crowded, so it's better to use three different pans for the 12 seeds than one large flat or milk carton. After planting the seeds, soak the soil with a mister. It's best to do this gently and thoroughly although no water should be left floating on the surface of the soil.

Continue to water the seeds whenever the soil tends to dry out—a gentle misting each day should be enough in most instances. The real danger to the beans is overwatering which can cause the germinating seeds to rot. Just keeping the soil moist rather than wet is fine.

You can also plant coffee beans in small plastic bags partially filled with soil. Plant the bean about ½ inch deep just as you would in a flat. Mist the soil until it's moist from top to bottom (it should never be soggy or mushy, though!). You can seal the bag with a rubber band. The advantage of this planting method is that it's particularly easy to transplant the seedling from the bag when the tiny plant begins to sprout. Generally, soil in an enclosed bag will stay moist for several weeks—another advantage. You may want to open the bag once a day to provide fresh air and to check on the moisture content of the soil. Never let it dry out. When the seedling begins to sprout, open the bag and place the growing plant where there's a lot of sun.

The seeds normally begin to sprout in about 25 to 40 days, although some have taken as long as a year. It'll be very tempting to take a look at the seeds or to touch them during this period. However strong your curiosity, *don't* disturb the seeds. They are very sensitive to touch during germination. Even when the seeds begin to push up through the soil, don't touch them.

Once they seem to be growing vigorously, you can either leave all the plantlets to grow as they are or you can choose the best plants and uproot the others. Actually, you don't have to destroy any plants, but you should take out the weaker plants from the pan so that they won't inhibit the growth of the stronger plants. You may try to transplant these weaker plants if you'd like, but they may not take root. Choosing the strongest plant is quite easy: its stem will be straighter and stronger than the others, the leaves will be developing more quickly, and the plant will seem more vital and fresh without any discoloration.

It's important to thin out the weaker plants to give the healthier plant a chance to spread its roots throughout the container. When the healthy plant has four leaves, you can transplant it to a 4-inch pot. The soil should be kept moist but never wet, so saturate the pot with a good watering whenever the soil begins to get dry. Never allow water to float on the soil surface. Heavy watering is essential in spring and summer while relatively light watering is sufficient in both fall and winter.

Since coffee plants don't like to be transplanted, leave the plant in the original pot for at least 9 months. At that time you can move it into an 8-inch pot where it will probably have enough room to grow for 2 years. However, a potbound coffee plant is miserable and responds by losing its leaves. If this happens, you may have to re-pot the plant no matter how short or long a time it's been in its new home. Try a pot one size larger.

Coffee plants require attention, but they aren't as difficult to grow as many other exotic plants. They prefer a sunny southern exposure with some shade in the summer. Frequent mistings and high humidity are great. The ideal temperature for a coffee plant is between 65° and 75°. Coffee plants don't like heavy winds and should be kept out of cold and warm drafts (heating ducts) at all times. The plants tend to grow in irregular shapes, and it's not going to hurt them if you decide to snip off an unruly branch or two to make the plant more attractive. You can also cut the plant back to force it to branch.

If you do, why not use this cutting to propagate another tree? The cutting of partially hardened wood (from the top of a 1-year-old plant)* often takes root when planted properly. Dip the bottom of the freshly cut tree tip in a rooting hormone such as *Hormidin* or *Rootone* and place it in moist sand. You can strip off any leaves which come in contact with the sand. Place the cutting in indirect light and mist it as frequently as possible since it is most likely to root in a humid atmosphere. Roots should begin to form in 6 to 12 weeks.

The coffee tree with its curly, deep-green foliage will be an exciting addition to any indoor garden. Although it grows well above 10 or 12 feet in a natural setting, no one should expect it to grow quite that tall in an apartment. As with most indoor, fruit-bearing trees, it's unlikely that the coffee plant will bloom. However, with attention and love it can live for many years giving you the enjoyment of growing one of nature's most beautiful trees.

---

* When cuttings from side branches are rooted, they grow horizontally. Their unusual configuration makes them a popular conversation piece.

## DIEFFENBACHIA *(Dumbcane)*

Dieffenbachia is commonly known as dumbcane since a toxic substance in its leaves, if chewed, causes temporary paralysis of the tongue. Yet these deep green leaves speckled with white and cream flecks make the dieffenbachia one of the most attractive house plants. Furthermore, it's a durable plant that can withstand a great deal of abuse. Although there are over 30 species of dieffenbachia, the following methods for starting this plant from scratch apply to most of them.

Dieffenbachia can be grown from cuttings taken from the growing tip (the top of the plant). With a sharp knife cut just under a node (or the spot from which a leaf once grew), about 4 to 6 inches below the tip of the plant. You can place this cutting in water or in moist sand. The stem should be placed 2 inches deep in the sand, which is a better rooting medium than water. Make sure that the sand is never allowed to dry out and mist the leaves frequently. Since water does evaporate from large leaves, you can trim them back to half their size by snipping off the ends of the leaves. Don't worry about the plant's appearance at this stage—it will be ugly! As long as the leaves and the sand are kept moist with frequent mistings, roots will begin to form at the base of the cutting in several weeks, certainly within 6 weeks. As soon as a healthy ball of roots has grown at the base of the plant (you can dig into the sand with your fingers to feel them), transplant the dieffenbachia into a 5-inch pot. Don't plant it any deeper than 2 inches and try to spread the roots evenly throughout the sterilized soil. Treat the new plant as you would an adult dieffenbachia. Most growers will tell you that cuttings taken in late spring and early summer are most successful.

At the base of a dieffenbachia you'll sometimes notice new growth developing. This is an offshoot which can be grown into another plant. All you have to do is to

# DIEFFENBACHIA

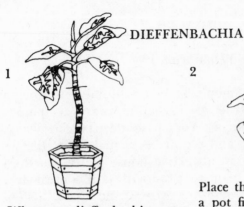

**1**

**2**

When a dieffenbachia gets leggy, cut off the top about 6 inches below the lowest leaf. Be sure to cut ½ inch below a white ring or node. Make a second cut through the stem 6 inches above the soil. Mark the stem between the two cuts with arrows showing which part was closest to the soil.

Place the top of the plant in a pot filled with sterile sand or in a large bowl filled with water. Wire mesh will keep the cutting from toppling over. Once the cutting has roots 6 to 8 inches long, plant it in a pot filled with sterilized soil.

**3**

**4**

Never throw the original plant away. The stub will grow into a new plant as long as it's kept moist and warm.

Cut the main stem into 4- to 8-inch sections which have at least two white rings encircling them. Dust the ends with powdered charcoal.

**5**

**6**

Sections of the stem grow well in water or sterile sand. If planted vertically, the head of the arrow should point down.

If planted horizontally, a section of the stem should never be planted any deeper than just under the surface of the sand. Sections planted like a log floating in water do well.

cut this shoot away from the parent plant with a sharp knife. Don't cut into the main stem but slide the blade down into the soil, separating the offshoot and some roots from the main plant. Pull this shoot, root ball, and clump of soil from the pot. Plant the offshoot in a 5-inch pot filled with sterilized soil. Try not to plant it any deeper than it was in the original pot. Soak the soil until it's thoroughly moist and cover the plant and pot with a plastic bag to keep the humidity high around it. Since the plant needs fresh air to grow, you should poke a few holes in the plastic. The plant should stay in this make-shift greenhouse until the roots take hold—usually about 2 weeks. Keep the "greenhouse" out of direct sunlight. Within 3 or 4 weeks the plant should have formed a very healthy root system and be growing well. At this stage you can remove the plastic cover and treat the new plant just as you would any other dieffenbachia.

Dieffenbachia often grows quite tall and becomes lanky. Some varieties look like palm trees with a tuft of leaves hanging from the top of the stem. While some growers find this attractive, many do not. If you fall into the latter group, don't despair. This tall, bare stem with limited leaves can be made into a number of very attractive, small dieffenbachia plants.

The procedure entails using the top of the plant to make one dieffenbachia, sections of the stem to make several new plants, and the base with the root system for another plant.

First, stake the stem of the plant with a bamboo cane. Let's start from the top. Decide how tall you'd like your leafy dieffenbachia to be. Let's say you want a plant 12 inches high. Make a diagonal cut with a sharp knife blade 12 inches below the top leaves. This cut should slant upwards cutting one third of the way into the stem. Remember you're not cutting off the top part of the plant; instead, you're deliberately wounding the plant for a specific purpose. (See pages 108–9 for illustration.)

You don't want this wound to heal, but you do want it to create roots. Place a piece of a broken wooden matchstick or a thick toothpick (you may have to use several) into the wound to make sure that it stays open. Do this carefully while supporting the stem with your hand so that it doesn't break off. You can support the plant with a long bamboo cane tied to the stem. Dust the open wound with a light application of rooting hormone. Now take a handful of damp sphagnum moss and cover the wound with it. Surround the entire stem with this moss. To keep the moss in place, wrap it with a 10-inch square piece of plastic tied at both ends with pieces of string. Although it's possible to do this by yourself, it helps to have a friend work with you. What you will end up with is a bulge on the stem of the plant. Check on the moisture content of the sphagnum moss each week by untying the upper string. If the moss is drying out, you should mist it until it's thoroughly soaked. Then tie the plastic back to the stem to keep the moisture in the moss.

With most plants you'll begin to notice roots forming from the wound in about 6 weeks. As soon as the roots are 6 inches long and filling in the "bulge" area, remove the plastic and cut off the stem with a sharp knife just below the roots. Don't disturb the fragile root system. Pot the new plant so that the sterilized soil is just above the new root system. There's your first plant!

Now, cut the stem just above a node (white circle) that's no more than 4 to 6 inches above the soil. Mark the severed cane with a pencil so you know which is the base end. Keep the soil moist around the stump and within 3 to 6 months you should see new growth. That's your second plant. But don't discard the stem which you've severed from the original plant.

Depending upon its length this stem can become 2 or even 10 new plants. The following three methods show how to get plants from this seemingly worthless "cane."

(1) Cut the stem into sections making sure that each section has at least two nodes (white circles around the stem) or leaf scars (spots from which leaves once grew). These sections can be as short as 4 inches or as long as 8. The important point is not the length but the number of nodes in the section. Dust the ends of the sections with powdered charcoal to prevent rotting. Place the sections horizontally in moist sand with half the stem exposed to the air so that it looks like a floating log. Keep the sections in a cool, dark place for about 6 to 8 weeks. Don't allow the sand to go dry. After 6 weeks, move the plants to a warmer spot or increase the temperature so it reaches 70° to 80°. Don't place the cuttings in the sun. Shoots should spring from the cutting. As soon as the shoots have three or four leaves, cut off the portion of the cane with shoots using a sharp knife. If the shoots have roots, pot them immediately and treat them as you would adult dieffenbachias. If the shoot doesn't have any roots, plant it in moist sand, perlite, vermiculite, or peat until it forms a root system. Then pot it in sterilized soil.

(2) Cut the stem into sections with two nodes on each section. Make sure you mark that part of the section that was closest to the roots of the parent plant. Place the sections in water so that the bottom of the cutting (the one which was nearest the roots of the parent plant) rests in 1 inch of water. Drip wax on the top of the cutting to seal the wound exposed to the air. Change the water twice a week until a root system forms. Then pot the plant in sterilized soil making sure not to plant it any deeper than it was resting in water.

(3) Cut the stem into sections with two nodes on each section. Once again, make sure you know which end is down—it's almost impossible to know unless you mark the cuttings. Fill a large plastic pot with either perlite,

peat, or vermiculite. Inside the large plastic pot, place a small clay pot which has been plugged with cork or covered with strapping tape on the bottom to prevent water from leaking through the drainage hole. This is the classic Forsyth pot (see page 197 for details). By keeping the clay pot filled with water, the surrounding mix will always be moist. Plant the sections at least 2 inches deep in the rooting medium, again making sure that the bottom part of the stem is used for this purpose. Within 6 to 8 weeks these cuttings should begin to root and show signs of growth as they send up new shoots. These sections can be potted in individual 5-inch pots as soon as they have a full root system.

Dieffenbachia is considered one of the hardiest indoor plants. It thrives best in bright indirect light but will survive in dimmer light as well. Don't place the plant in direct sunshine. Since the plant has large leaves, try to keep these clean with frequent sponge baths. No matter how thick the plant's leaves, sponge gently and support them with your other hand as you wipe off the dust and grime. Since the plant thrives on humidity, take it into the shower with you from time to time. Admittedly, with the larger plants this is impossible, but you can set the pot on a tray filled with pebbles and water to increase the surrounding humidity. Although the plant grows quickly, avoid frequent repotting. If you want to move a dieffenbachia into new living quarters, you'll have the best luck with this in late spring or early summer. Dieffenbachia has a voracious appetite and requires frequent feeding, two times a month from early spring to late fall and once a month the rest of the year. Normal temperatures in the average apartment suit the plant well. It does nicely in temperatures of 72° to 75° with a drop of 10° at night.

One mistake which can kill a dieffenbachia: overwatering! Between thorough waterings, when water drains from the bottom drainage holes, allow the surface of the soil to dry for 2 days. Even though the surface will be dry, the soil underneath remains moist for a day or two. After the second day, give the plant a good soaking with tepid water. Depending upon the season and the indoor temperature, you can get by with watering the plant as infrequently as once every 2 weeks. The only way to tell when to water is to feel the soil in the pot with your fingers. If the upper 2 inches of soil have been dry for 2 days that tells you it's time to water again. During a summer heat wave you may have to water the plant twice a week. No one can give you an exact schedule for watering any plant, but you can be sure of killing your hardy dieffenbachia if it continually has "wet feet."

Chances are that this lovely foliage plant will live for years with its long leaves fanning out from its thick stem. Whether it looks like a fluffy shrub or a piece of cane with a tuft of hair on top, it's one of the more graceful large-leafed plants. Displayed in a decorative tub, the dieffenbachia can make an entire room seem to breathe life and good health.

# DRACAENA

The island of Tenerife in the Canary Islands was once covered with "dragon trees," one of the 50 species of dracaena. These trees exude a dark-red sap said to be "dragon's blood," so highly prized in many cultures as a cure-all of illness that it was sold for its weight in gold. Today, there is one large dragon tree left on Tenerife. Probably several thousand years old, it is protected as a national monument.

Several species of dracaena make superb house plants.

# AIR LAYERING (DRACAENA)

**1**

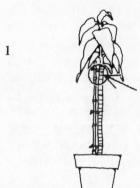

When your dieffenbachia, dracaena, *Monstera deliciosa*, croton, schefflera, or ti plant gets
leggy, support it with a thin
cane.

**2**

Make a diagonal cut about a
third of the way through the
stem at any point you select
below the bottom leaf. Use a
sharp knife, cut deeply, but
don't cut off the top of the
plant.

**3**

Make sure that the wound
doesn't heal by propping it
open with pieces of a toothpick or a wooden matchstick.
Dust the wound with a rooting hormone such as *Rootone*
or *Hormidin*.

**4**

Wrap a 9-inch-square piece of
clear plastic around the stem.
Tie it firmly around the base
of the wound. Pack the plastic
with a handful of moist
sphagnum moss.

 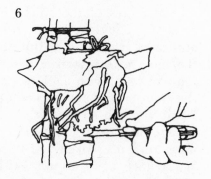

Tie the top of the plastic tightly around the stem so that the wound is surrounded by a bulge of wet moss. Untie the top twine weekly to check on the dampness of the moss. If it's drying out, pour warm water over it.

When the bulge begins to swell with growing roots (usually within 6 to 8 weeks), cut off the top of the plant just below the bottom roots. Plant it so that the top roots are just below the soil surface. *Never throw the original plant away.* It will sprout new growth if kept moist and warm.

The compact *Dracaena sanderiana* has short, thin, ribbonlike leaves with 4 to 6 inches of stem. You can cut off its growing tip and root it in moist sand. Both the *Dracaena fragrans massangeana* and the *Dracaena marginata* are among the most popular house plants. Both contain many potential plants for the daring indoor gardener.

Support the Dracaena with a bamboo cane—a tomato prop variety. Take a sharp knife and make an upward incision about 12 inches from the growing tip of the plant. Cut under a node well under any foliage. This cut should be at an angle slanting one third of the way through the stem between two nodes. Be sure to support the cane as you make the cut since it will snap off with too much pressure. Insert a wooden matchstick or several pieces of toothpicks into the wound to keep it open. Dust it lightly with *Rootone* (a rooting hormone) and cover it with a handful of damp sphagnum moss (let the moss soak in warm water for an hour). Secure the moss in place with a 10-inch square piece of plastic. Tie the bottom and top of the plastic in place with string. Untie the top string each week to make sure that the sphagnum moss is damp. If it starts to dry out, mist the moss until it's soaked and tie the string around the stem again. (See illustration.) Within 10 to 12 weeks roots should begin growing from the wound into the surrounding moss. As soon as the moss is filled with a healthy root system, cut off the top of the plant with a sharp knife just underneath the roots. Pot the new plant in a separate pot and treat it as you would the original parent plant.

Next, cut the remaining stem back to a height of 4 to 6 inches.* That tiny stub will grow into another plant. You can also make a number of plants from the remaining cane. Cut the stem into 6-inch sections. You can plant each section in a Forsyth pot (see page 197), but make sure that the cutting is placed in the soil with the right end down. The end which was nearest the roots of the parent plant should always be planted in the soil. Place the cutting about 2 inches deep in moist sand or vermiculite. The dracaena cuttings should begin to root within 6 to 12 weeks. Once they have a healthy root system and several leaves, plant them in individual pots. This classic method of "radical surgery" converts one dracaena into many others. Your odds of being successful are high—even if you lose one or two of the cuttings, you should come out ahead (especially in the spring).

Each variety of dracaena has its unique characteristics and needs, but in general they are easy plants to take care

---

* Be sure to mark the base of the stem with a pencil so you will know which end was nearest the roots.

of. The soil should be moist; as soon as it begins to dry out, give the plant a thorough soaking. Don't mist the plants. They like high humidity, which can be provided by placing the pots on a tray filled with pebbles and water. The water should not touch the bottom of the pot or root rot will occur. High temperatures are tolerated well by the dracaena, but it will also survive in the 65° to 70° range. Good light in an east or west window as well as monthly fertilizing will encourage full and fast growth.

Cleve Backster's unusual experiments using a lie detector and a dracaena suggested that plants and man can communicate. Backster noticed that his dracaena responded to a mental threat to burn it by showing a response on the polygraph recording similar to one a person experiencing stress would show. With a little time and attention, your plants can respond to you, providing you with pleasure for many, many years.

## GRAPE

The mountainous Douro region of northern Portugal seems suited only to mountain goats and soaring hawks. However, over the past several centuries the inhabitants of this forbidding region have constructed terraces on the steep slopes. Sometimes using picks and other times using dynamite, they have broken into the mountain and created pockets in which grape vines are able to grow. From this hostile region comes the world's great port wines.

On the parched volcanic island of Lanzarote lying just west of the Sahara desert, you'll find acres of arid earth which looks like they have been devastated by high-intensity bombing. Actually, the indentations in the earth are filled with a porous powdery rock known as *picon.* It absorbs moisture at night and allows plants growing within it to survive for months and even years without any rain. The plants grown here are grapes. The vines cling to the dusty, gray soil and produce a delicious fruit used in making a kind of Malvasia wine.

The grape vine is one of the most versatile and rugged plants imaginable. Each variety can withstand a specific kind of abuse. Some can be crusted with salt from a nearby sea without suffering. Others will survive freezing winters popping from dormancy into full growth in early spring.

You can start your own grape vine from scratch. The seedless grapes with their clear, juicy flesh are naturally useless to the indoor gardener. However, the plump variety, often with a rich red skin, contains seeds which can be planted indoors. Suck the pulp from around the seeds and wash them in warm water until they're completely clean. Place the seeds in a plastic bag or jar partially filled with slightly damp peat moss and store in the refrigerator (not the freezer) for 3 months (the ideal temperature falls in the 33° to 40° range). Since this is a long wait, use as many seeds as possible to increase your chances of getting one of them to germinate when they're finally planted. Work with at least 50 to 100 seeds—that's not all that many grapes to eat!

After the make-believe winter, plant the seeds ⅛ to ¼ inch deep in sterilized soil lightened with peat or vermiculite and mist the soil until it's thoroughly moist. Place the flat in as warm a spot as possible to speed up germination. Use soil heating cables if available. Cover the pot or flat with plastic or glass to keep the humidity high, but lift the cover each day to allow air to circulate around the seeds and to make sure that the soil is not drying out.

When the seeds begin to sprout after several weeks, you can remove the cover and move the plantlets into bright light. Continue to keep the soil moist. If the pot seems crowded with the plants touching each other, it's best to thin them out by snipping some out with a scissors. Don't pull any plants out by their roots since you'll disturb the remaining plants. After the seedlings have developed several leaves, transplant them to individual pots.

Since grape vines grow best in very bright light, a southern exposure is highly recommended. Keep the plants warm and somewhat on the dry side in the summer. Allow the soil to dry out for a day or two between thorough waterings. With warmth, bright light, and good soakings whenever needed, you'll find that the grape vine will grow rapidly.

The growing period lasts only from early spring to early fall (sometimes late fall). Fertilize the plant twice a month during the active growing months. You can train the vine to curl around windows or up a stick by allowing the tendrils at the end of the vine to find support, whether it's tacks nailed into the woodwork or string wrapped around a pole.

The vine should begin to turn yellow in the fall when it goes into dormancy. Gradually reduce watering and cut the vine back to about 10 inches high. This pruning may seem drastic, but it won't hurt the plant a bit. Store the pot in a cool, airy spot until early spring. Water it only once a month during the dormant period. In February soak the soil thoroughly and place the pot in a warm window once again. New growth will appear as the plant is exposed to warmth, water, and bright light.*

The woody vine makes an interesting seasonal foliage plant and requires very little attention. It's relatively free of pests and is quite hardy.

* These plants do not always survive apartment conditions which cannot duplicate the outdoors. It's worth a try anyway!

## KUMQUAT

Kumquats are small evergreen trees which grow freely in the subtropical regions of southeastern Asia. From the small white starlike flowers appear miniature golden fruits, about the size of a small orange. They have long been a favorite fruit in China.

Kumquats can be found in many grocery stores from November until June although they sometimes spoil before reaching the market in late May. In choosing kumquats, try to pick out firm fruits with no sign of shriveling and without blemishes. If a kumquat is not quite ripe, you should let it mature in a warm area in your apartment.

Unlike either oranges or lemons the kumquat has a sweet skin which adds a lovely flavor to the tart pulp inside. Always eat the skin with the juicy fruit to get the best taste possible. Don't discard the seeds from kumquats because they can be grown into beautiful indoor plants. You'll find from one to five seeds in each fruit.

As with citrus fruits, you should never allow the seeds to dry out. The longer a seed is allowed to dry, the less chance there is of getting it to grow. Therefore, take the seed directly from the fruit and plant it in sterilized soil about $\frac{1}{2}$ inch deep. You can plant several seeds in the same pot until they begin to grow. Be sure to keep the soil moist—this is the most important condition to start the seeds growing.

Once the seeds are several inches tall, you can move them into individual pots. Keep them in a warm, yet airy spot in the apartment. Cool temperatures in winter are fine since this plant is tuned to a period of chills. However, bright sun is always needed. The kumquat will thrive in the direct light of a sunny window (southern exposure).

This is a striking foliage plant with dark green glossy leaves that have an exotic appeal. Wash the foliage with warm water frequently to keep it free of dust. The leaves stay fresh and especially vibrant with constant misting in dry winter conditions. Pruning won't hurt the plant, but do it in the summer when the plant will fill out in foliage.

The kumquat is one of the most pleasing potted plants. If you can get it to bloom, you'll be entranced with the sweet scent exuded by the white flowers. Even without blooming, the kumquat is a superb house plant. Treat it with the same care and love as you do your grapefruit tree, and you'll be surprised at how much deep-green color it will lend your apartment for many years.

## LOQUAT

Although often nicknamed the "Japanese plum," the loquat is really Chinese in origin. A member of the rose family, it makes a lovely ornamental evergreen shrub. In the wild the tree reaches a height of 10 to 25 feet. When young it is covered with soft, downy leaves. As the tree matures, the leaves turn a deep green and seem leathery in texture. The growth of the branches is often so symmetrical that the loquat seems to be self-pruning in nature. The tree's flowers, which rarely bloom indoors, are yellowish white and have a sweet, seductive scent.

The loquat fruit is about the size of a large cherry or a small apricot. It is either pear-shaped or round depending upon the variety. The downy skin ranges from light yellow to bright orange in color. Loquats must be picked when fully ripe and they'll keep well for up to 6 weeks. Inside the fuzzy skin you'll find a juicy cream-colored flesh that most people find delicious. Loquats are sold from late March to early May in fine stores noted for excellent produce departments.

The indoor gardener will be interested in the hard, brown seeds inside the fruit. Loquats have from one to four of these shiny, oblong seeds which are usually about ½ to ¾ inch long. Remove the seeds from the fruit and wash them in warm water until they're completely clean.

Plant the seeds in sterilized soil about ½ inch deep. Mist the soil until it's moist throughout and keep the pot or flat in a warm spot. A plastic or glass cover over the pot will maintain a high level of humidity around the seeds. Never let the soil dry out.

As soon as the seedlings break through the surface of the soil, move them into bright light and take off the plastic cover. Continue to keep the soil moist. Once a loquat is growing steadily in late spring and early summer, you can allow the soil to go dry for a day or two between waterings. However, mist the plant frequently to keep the foliage healthy and clean. The loquat also appreciates occasional foliage baths in warm water or sharing a shower with you.

In ideal growing conditions of warmth, light, and moisture, your loquat may grow as much as 1 foot each year. Each time a plant grows this much, you should repot it into a larger pot or tub using fresh sterilized soil. The best time to repot a loquat is in late winter or early spring as it enters a new growing phase during these longer days.

The loquat is one of the most cherished ornamental trees. Not quite as demanding as many other exotic plants, it's still a challenge to the green thumb and may well end up as one of your favorite indoor plants.

# MACADAMIA

The macadamia tree is a subtropical evergreen originally from Australia. It produces a hard-shelled nut with a core similar to a filbert. These tough nuts are sold in many grocery stores as a specialty item. As long as the light-brown nuts are still intact with their deep-brown shell, they make interesting potential plants for the indoor gardener. Macadamia nuts are freshest in the fall although they can be planted as long as 9 months after they've been harvested. If you want to store the nuts, place them in an airtight jar in the refrigerator. You can plant them months later.

Fresh macadamia nuts are generally sold in packages of about twenty-five. Only some of these nuts will grow into healthy trees. To separate the good from the bad, drop all of the nuts into a basin filled with hot water (120° to 130°). Those seeds which sink to the bottom make good potential trees while the ones which float on top will not germinate—the latter should be cracked open and eaten. Usually, about 80 percent of the nuts in any package will sink and can be planted. Always plant five or six nuts for each tree desired since some seeds will not take root. If you have trouble finding fresh macadamia nuts, write to Produce Specialties, Inc., 732 Market Court, Los Angeles, California 90021. Enclose a stamped, self-addressed envelope for a reply. They will tell you where to obtain unusual fruits and nuts in your area.

The odds are good that in any package of fresh nuts you'll find several that will root. Professional growers insist that if you crack the dark brown coating of a macadamia nut to encourage quick growth, you increase the odds of fungus growth. If you want to take the chance (I suggest you do), go ahead and crack the shell. This will expose the white flesh inside and will allow water to get to the seed quickly. (Growers suggest instead that you

# MACADAMIA

1

Drop macadamia nuts into a basin filled with hot water. The ones that sink can be grown into trees.

2

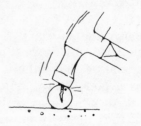

Crack open the nuts which sank by using a hammer to break through the tough outer shell.

3

Soak the nut in warm water for 3 hours before dusting the open crack with rooting hormone.

4

Plant the nuts ½ inch deep in moist sterilized soil.

5

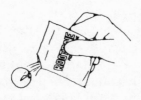

Keep the soil moist and warm until light pink shoots spring from the soil.

6

When the plant is four to six inches high, transplant it into its own pot.

soak the seed in hot water for 2 hours, or sand off some of the thick shell with sandpaper.)

Crack a nut by placing it on a very hard surface and by giving it a firm tap on its side with a hammer. A few of the nuts will explode, so eat these as a snack since they won't grow. Eventually, you'll know just how hard to hit the nut to crack it. Remember, you're not trying to break off the shell—just to split it open slightly. As the nut cracks, it makes a sharp splitting sound. Soak the freshly cracked nuts for several hours in warm water.

Dust the opening of the crack with a light coating of rooting hormone after removing the nut from the water. This hormone will kill most fungi that could kill the germinating seed. Place the nut ½ inch deep in moist sterilized soil which should be kept moist and warm. In several weeks the nut will begin to swell. Finally, a white root will shoot downward into the soil while a fuzzy stem appears through the surface of the soil.

After the seedling reaches a height of 4 to 6 inches, transplant it into an individual 8-inch pot. Keep the soil moist and warm, and place the plants where they can receive sunlight. Repot the tree whenever it gets too large for its present home. Fertilize it once a month during active growing periods.

Macadamia nuts are quite inexpensive and from a package bought in the store you should get several small trees. They make intriguing indoor foliage plants with hollylike leaves although they rarely bloom with their characteristic white clusters of flowers.

## PAPAYA *(Pawpaw)*

When scientists in Great Britain first saw a stuffed platypus imported from Australia they roared, thinking that it was a practical joke. After all, here was a furry animal with a broad fleshy bill similar to that of a duck. And, yes, it did lay eggs. But it was also a mammal which suckled its young. In a way the papaya is to the plant world what the platypus is to the animal kingdom.

The papaya is indeed a ridiculous-looking plant. At maturity it looks like a large stalk with a toupee of deep-green leaves similar in shape to those of an oak or maple, but the leaves are gigantic in comparison. The papaya's unusual appearance is matched only by its bizarre sex habit. It is actually capable of changing from one sex to another in its lifetime!

Under ideal conditions the papaya grows rapidly. At the end of a year it may be 10 or 12 feet tall when it bears an odd-looking fruit that clings to the top of the stalk under the leaves. Each tree bears many papayas weighing from 1 to 20 pounds. Some are about the size of a small grapefruit while others are much larger and resemble a gourd. They ripen from a dark green to a light yellow. Papayas are now available in many stores throughout the United States at any time of year. Choose a fruit that is yellow and slightly soft.

Papaya is a fascinating exotic plant to grow from scratch. Cut the fruit in two from the fat end to the narrow end where you'll see a tiny bit of the stem where the fruit was attached to the tree. Cutting through the outer skin with a sharp knife is very easy, and you don't have to worry about damaging a pit since each papaya has hundreds of small seeds in its center. These look like tiny miniature raisins enclosed in a slimy clear sack. Scoop the seeds out of the salmon-colored fruit onto absorbent paper. Squeeze each seed between your thumb and forefinger until the sack pops and the seed slides out. Any outdoor gardener will tell you that a papaya seed has the rough, wrinkled appearance of a beet seed and is the same dark brown color.

Although many farmers in the West Indies plant only two or three seeds to get one plant, you'd better use all the seeds from the fruit. The task of separating the seed from the slimy coating takes patience and will pay off in the end, since from a hundred or more seeds you may only get three or four to germinate.

Seeds from a papaya can be planted immediately or allowed to dry out and planted later. Plant the seeds about ½ inch deep and 1 inch apart in a flat of sterilized soil. Cover them with a thin layer of shredded sphagnum moss. It's extremely important to use sterilized soil since papaya seedlings are susceptible to "damping off," a soil-borne fungus disease which causes the lower portion of the stem to collapse. (See page 195). Mist the newly planted seeds until the soil is thoroughly moist but not soggy. If you can supply some bottom heat, this will help the seeds to germinate. Special heating pads and coils are available from garden centers and nurseries. Seeds generally take from 2 to 6 weeks to sprout, but don't be discouraged if it takes longer. Continue to keep the soil moist and warm until the seeds begin to split open, pushing the soil upward as the seedlings emerge in a pale green arc.

Once a papaya is growing, it grows rapidly. When it reaches the height of 4 inches, you should transplant it into a 6-inch pot. As the papaya matures, gradually increase the amount of direct sunshine until it's in full sun. Warmth (60° and above) and light encourage quick growth, and therefore frequent repotting of this healthy plant will be essential. Papayas sometimes survive occasional chills and drafts, but try to avoid these if possible. Papayas like rich soil and lots of water in spring and summer. However, never let the roots of the plant stand in water. Provide a drainage dish under the pot for excess water to drain. It's almost impossible to overwater this plant on hot days in the middle of July and August but during the winter watering can be cut back considerably. Don't prune or mist these plants. Unfortunately, papayas don't live longer than 3 or 4 years, nor do they bear fruit. Papayas are also sensitive to pollution—although you may do everything right, papayas can be destroyed by poisonous gases in the environment.

The papaya is nevertheless a fascinating plant to grow from scratch. While experimenting with its seeds, enjoy the perfumy sweet fruit which is enhanced when sprinkled with lemon or lime. It's a tropical mainstay filled with vitamins A and C. South American women use the fruit as a facial. After removing the flesh, rub the inside of the skin over your face. Allow the enzyme in the juice to remain on the skin for 5 or 10 minutes. Afterwards, rinse it off with warm water. As strange as it may sound, the enzyme (papain) found in papayas is used in meat tenderizers!

## QUINCE

Once extremely popular in the northeastern part of the United States, the quince is now little known. The quince tree produces an irregular, pear-shaped fruit known as "golden apple of the Hesperides." It has been used to make lotions, perfumes, medicine, and even wine. No wonder that the Greeks and Romans considered the quince endowed with mystical powers to enhance love, happiness, and fertility.

The unusual quince can be found in some specialty shops from October to December. You may have to ask the produce manager to order some for you. The fruit has a woolly, yellow skin with a distinctive, strong aroma. Choose large and smooth fruits without any spots, bruises, or worm holes. Cut off the skin and remove the core surrounding the seeds. The meat of the quince tends to be firm and very tart. Most people prefer cooking the pulp to make jellies.

Save the seeds after you take them from the core and store them in a plastic bag partially filled with moist (not soggy) peat moss. Seal the bag tightly. The seeds should be cooled in your refrigerator for 2 to 3 months at about 40°.

After removing the seeds from the refrigerator, plant them ½ inch deep in sterilized soil. Place the pot or flat on top of soil heating cables or on a cookie tray resting on a radiator. This will speed up germination. Keep the soil constantly moist, and within several weeks you'll see young sprouts appear. After they have six green leathery leaves, transplant them to individual 3-inch pots. As they mature, gradually move them into larger pots.

This tree goes through a dormant period in winter and thrives best when placed in the ground outdoors. Like the ordinary apple, the quince produces lovely pink and white flowers outdoors. However, this is very rare in apartments. Enjoy this unusual indoor tree for its unique personality, foliage, and symbolic meaning. Perhaps it will bring love and happiness into your household as it did to so many people who worshipped it in the past.

## TAMARIND  (Indian date)

The tamarind tree grows wild in the arid tropical regions of Ethiopia. Small green leaves tinged with yellow and red cover its branches forming a 70- to 80-foot canopy over the parched earth below. These leaves are used in making dyes and in flavoring native curries. Sometimes the tree bursts into bloom with exquisite orange-veined, yellow flowers.

Although the tamarind tree is unlikely to bloom indoors with its fragrant scent, it can make an attractive foliage plant if properly cared for. To grow a tamarind you'll have to stop by at an oriental food store and pick up a plastic-wrapped package of this podlike fruit.

These pods look like chocolate-covered string beans and have a brittle shell with bulges in it. If you break through the outer covering, you'll find a sticky pulp inside which looks, feels, and tastes like the center of a Fig Newton cookie. Surrounded by this pasty pulp are flat shiny beans which can germinate into tamarind trees.

Remove the beans from the pulp and wash them in warm water until they're completely clean. You'll find from one to six of these hard, brown beans about the size of a lima bean in each of the pods. Soak the bean for 24 hours in warm water before potting it ¼ inch deep in sterilized soil. You may want to plant about three or four seeds to a 4-inch pot. Mist the soil until it's thoroughly moist. Cover the pot with plastic or glass to keep the humidity high.

Although the seeds can be kept in a dark spot, try to keep them as warm as possible to encourage quick root growth. The seeds normally begin to sprout within 6 to 8 weeks, although this varies considerably. Don't give up too quickly! Just keep the soil moist and warm at all times.

As soon as the thick, cream-colored stem emerges from the soil, remove the cover from the pot allowing air to circulate freely around the plantlet. Gradually move the seedling into bright light. Continue to mist it frequently and don't let it get chilled since it adores warmth and responds with vigorous growth. Remember to mist the plant out of direct light! The shoot emerges with the seed, splits to shed it, and grows paired leaves on a pale green stem. Once leaves seem to be growing vigorously from the shoot, reduce watering slightly. If several seedlings are growing in one pot, they should be transplanted to individual pots as soon as they have several leaves and a healthy root system.

Give this plant a warm, bright location in your apartment. The larger the plant, the more it can withstand slightly dry conditions. Cut down on water during the winter and provide cooler indoor temperatures. Never place the tamarind in a drafty spot or it will drop leaves and die. The plant should have plenty of room to expand as it grows. Repot whenever it gets crowded by moving it into a slightly larger pot in the spring. Fertilize the tamarind during active growing periods from early spring to early fall.

This is an unusual plant that is rarely found in the United States. It makes a good conversation piece and can be a unique foliage plant for someone interested in exotica.

## TI PLANT

Many plants are believed to be endowed with mystical power. Throughout much of the western world the mandrake (or mandragora) was assumed to have magical powers in its human-shaped root. Some American Indians worshipped peyote, believing the luminous personality they met during hallucinogenic visions to be a deity. In Polynesia many natives believed the ti plant could ward off evil. It has therefore become a symbol of love, life, and luck.

This lovely foliage plant is a poor man's dracaena. In fact, it's sometimes called "common dracaena." The plant supports 12- to 18-inch palmlike leaves from a slender cane trunk. The leaves tend to be deep red or dark green edged in light red. In Hawaii the leaves are used as dishes at a luau and they also cover the hips of swaying hula girls. Lashed against the water the leaves make enough noise to scare fish into waiting nets. Leaves were once held above the head to indicate surrender and used as a sign of royal power, from which developed the standards carried high by soldiers marching at the side of their leader or king.

Pieces of the cane are now sold in many grocery stores as a novelty item. While many novelty items are worthless, this one is an exception. You'll find that the ends of the cane have been sealed with wax. Scrape it off and place the piece of cane in water—either vertically or horizontally. In both instances only half the cane should be submerged. Tepid water increases the chances of quick growth and should be changed frequently, at least three times a week.* However, never change the position of the log or the water level. The piece of cane should be placed in a warm spot in bright but not direct sunlight. In 6 to 8 weeks the cane will begin to sprout light white growth from nodes on the outer edge. When the sprouts are 2 or more inches long, plant the cane in sterilized soil lightened by additional peat. Do not use soil which contains perlite, as it has minute traces of fluoride in it. The cane should be in the same position it was in during the growth period. Cover the plant completely and soak the soil around it until it's thoroughly moist. Plant it in a 4-inch pot. You'll have to transplant it often since the plant can reach a height of 3 feet under ideal growing conditions.

The secret to getting this fine foliage plant to grow well is high humidity. Keep the soil moist, mist the leaves often, and place the pot on a tray filled with pebbles

* Ti plants react badly to fluoride. Try to use distilled water throughout the entire growth cycle.

and water. The water in the tray should never touch the bottom of the pot. The plant prefers the highest temperature possible in the apartment—it will survive in temperatures of 60° to 85°. Bright light with no more than 4 hours of direct sunlight a day is ideal. As long as the plant is kept out of cool drafts and away from chilling windows, it will remain attractive.

Most ti plants grow 2 to 3 feet tall. Sometimes, they will reach a height of 6 feet indoors. You can cut off the top 12 inches of the plant and place it in water. Water should be warm and changed as frequently as possible. Charcoal in the glass will keep the water from going stale. Within several weeks the cutting should sprout roots and can then be potted in a 7-inch pot or larger.

The stem of a healthy 3- to 4-year-old plant can also be cut with a sharp knife into 4- to 6-inch sections (see illustration on page 108). Each of these pieces of cane will look like the one you bought in the grocery store. Plant the sections horizontally after dusting the ends with powdered charcoal to prevent rot. Soil should be a mixture of potting soil and peat. Half of the piece of cane should be above the surface of the soil. Soak the soil thoroughly and keep it moist at all times although it should never be soggy. A humid environment and high temperature will increase the chances of new growth. Each section will grow into a healthy ti plant.

You'll find ti plants to be impressive foliage plants. Although they will blossom with light pinkish purple blooms under ideal conditions, this is relatively rare indoors. Whether it blossoms or not, the ti has always been a favorite, and is sure to enhance your indoor plant collection.

# Chapter IV

# Plants for the Deep-Green Thumb

Eventually, every indoor gardener wants to undertake the challenge of growing exotic and delicate plants that demand skill, lots of patience, and meticulous attention.

Many of the plants included in this chapter should not be classified as indoor plants at all. They are best suited to the plains of Australia or the rough hilly islands of the West Indies. However, it is possible to grow them in a brownstone apartment or in the living room of a house in a suburb of Milwaukee. But it's not easy!

A few of the plants are commonly found in retail florist shops and in many of your friends' apartments. However, the method of starting them from scratch can be quite unusual and equally difficult. For instance, in this chapter you'll discover how to grow ferns from spores.

The key to success with these difficult plants is to begin with more potential plants than you expect to have in the end. As an example, you may get only one large guava plant from a hundred miniscule seeds. But that one plant will be worth all 99 failures. Good luck!

## BANANA

Bananas are among the most exotic plants in their natural setting. In the Orotava Valley of Tenerife in the Canary Islands, 8 million banana trees grow along hillsides that are protected from the occasional heavy winds by gray brick walls. The lush green of these plants is set off by the brilliant reds of poinsettias growing to a height of 8 to 10 feet. Bananas are one of the most important crops on the island.

Bananas are not really trees at all. They are large herbs with lovely thick leaves rising from the ground in a sheath which simulates a trunk. These leaves, curling up from a sucker in the earth, grow 8 to 10 feet tall and can take anywhere from 12 to 14 months to mature. The fruit grows from a fertilized stalk that hangs down in an awkward position with the bananas growing in a seemingly upside-down angle. The large clumps of bananas are cut off the plant when they're still green and are allowed to mature en route to major markets.

The banana is a difficult plant to grow indoors because it requires much sunlight and space. The key to success is plenty of warmth and moisture.

After fruiting, banana trees are cut down. Outwardly, it looks as if the plant has died—and the parent plant *has* died. However, new suckers appear along the side where the old plant once stood. This slight change in position explains why banana trees rarely can be found in straight rows. The natives whimsically point out that bananas are the only trees which have "learned to walk."

Banana trees probably first grew in Southeast Asia. They have been recognized as one of the most valuable fruits in man's short history. They were certainly recognized for their delicious flavor as early as 500 B.C. when artists depicted them on the sides of caves in India. Many societies have considered bananas as sacred, calling them "fruits of paradise" and "fruits of knowledge." Their peculiar way of dying and sending up new trees led philosophers to compare them to a man's life—when a man's life's work is done, he dies.

The bananas you see in your local grocery store contain aborted seeds. They have been bred very skillfully so that the fruit is more appetizing. The elimination of seeds in fruit is considered very desirable by most growers. However, for the indoor gardener this creates a problem. How do you grow bananas if you don't have any seeds? Unfortunately, you don't. At least not from the bananas sold in supermarkets.

Instead, you have to write for seeds from Geo. W. Park Seed Company, Greenwood, South Carolina 29647. This company generally has seeds available for the indoor gardener who wants to grow an unusual plant in a "hostile" or unnatural environment. If you're still undaunted, why not give it a try? Order seeds as far in advance as possible. Ideally, they should arrive in early spring. The seeds have a hard coating with a scar (they look like rice kernels or small black nuts). Nick this outer coating with a nail file and soak the seed for a full day in warm water. Nicking the seed is not easy, and you may want to use sandpaper to remove a tiny portion of each side of the seed without digging into the core itself.

Since banana plants react badly to being transplanted, you should plant the seeds directly in a large wooden tub which will be their permanent home. The bottom of an old wine barrel or a large wooden waste paper basket make good pots for prospective banana plantations. Be sure to bore holes in the bottom so that excess water will drain out. Place the tub on a drainage pan filled with rocks or marbles. Large wooden tubs need lots of crocking—at least 3 inches at the bottom of the barrel. Fill the gaps in the crocks with coarse drainage material. Then fill the tub with sterilized potting soil leaving 1½ inches at the top for easy watering. Ideally, the soil temperature should be between 75° and 85°, which is very high for most apartments. Electric heating cables (available at some florist shops) can be wrapped around the tub, or it can be placed by a radiator. Plant the seed about ¼ inch under the soil with the scar up. Water the soil until it's completely moist without being soggy. In order to help maintain the high temperature needed for seed germination, place the tub in full sun. Without a southern exposure in your apartment this may be impossible. You'll have to rely on heating cables or a radiator. Under no circumstances should the temperature drop below 65°.

Seeds will sometimes sprout within 50 days, although some seeds take as long as a year to germinate. (Second thoughts?) When seedlings finally appear, move the tub into a slightly shady spot until they seem to be growing well. Gradually move the plant back into full sun. With luck, this will be sometime in the summer when the plant can get the "deep tan" it hungers for. Keep the soil moist at all times. Sponge the leaves to keep them clean and mist them as often as possible. This is a high-humidity plant. When cleaning leaves, use water at room temperature and support them with your hand so that they don't crack or break. Whenever the temperature is sweltering, open a window so that your plant will get fresh air.

Under ideal conditions a banana tree will grow to be 3 to 4 feet tall by the end of the summer, and will appreciate being fertilized during active growth. Feed it once every 4 weeks in the summer and once every 2 months in the winter with a liquid or water-soluble fertilizer. Cut down on the water in winter and try to get by on a "low-calorie" routine. Assuming that you've been able to grow the plant this far, you've already proven that you have a deep-green thumb.

If your plant makes it through its second spring and summer, it may once again get the full attention of direct sunlight. At this time you may see suckers appearing at the base of the banana tree. Of course, suckers may not appear for several years. Suckers spring from buds on the banana root (rhizome) which can be divided into 7- to 10-pound sections. Each section should contain two suckers. Each "suckered" section of root will become a mature banana tree. Let them dry for 2 or 3 days. Plant them in a 20-inch pot and treat as you would any ordinary, exotic, nearly impossible-to-grow tropical plant. In transplanting, try not to alter the plant soil level. The soil should come up to the same place on the plant as it did before you cut it from its mother.

Banana trees represent one of the ultimate challenges to the indoor gardener who is unlucky enough to be without a warm greenhouse. Whether or not the challenge is worth accepting depends mainly on your desire to grow an unusual, exotic, rarely seen plant and a willingness to foot the cost of high heating bills!

## COCONUT PALM

The coconut palm probably originated in Cocos Island west of Panama. In tropical regions the tree grows to a height of 80 feet and can produce as many as 200 nuts in a single season. The coconut is the second largest seed in the world, surpassed in size only by the Seychelles nut, which can weigh as much as 40 pounds. Each coconut is a potential palm.

However, the hairy brown coconuts you see in most grocery stores are just a part of the coconut which you'd find clustered at the top of a palm. The brown husk with delicious white coconut meat within is absolutely useless as a seed from which you could grow a tree. You can sometimes find whole coconuts displayed in some oriental markets, tucked in a corner of a specialty food store, and possibly hidden in a friend's suitcase after a trip to Florida. But, whole coconuts are difficult to find. Assuming that you discover one, you should be warned that your chances of getting it to germinate are one in four.

If you're willing to face those bleak odds, here's how to foster the large nut's growth on its way to becoming a living palm. First, notice that the outer husk or shell is very thick. To help the nut absorb water, sandpaper the hull until much of it is removed (do this on the sides of the nut). Since each nut varies in size, use your judgment to determine how long to scrape the sides. You don't want to go all the way through the husk to the core.

Lay the nut on its side in a large tub filled with a mixture of sterilized soil and sharp sand. The fat end of the nut has "eyes" from which the sprouting palm will emerge. These eyes should be facing upwards, and the fat end must be slightly higher than the narrow end— a 10° angle is perfect. Cover all of the nut except the upper 1-inch portion with sterilized soil. Soak the soil until it's thoroughly moist and place the pot in a very warm spot. Never let the soil dry out; mist the exposed part of the nut each day with tepid water. The keys to success: high temperature, moisture, and misting.

If you're really lucky, you'll notice a sprout emerging from an eye within 3 to 4 months. Many nuts take as long as a year to show signs of first growth. And three out of four nuts never sprout at all. Yes, this is a challenging plant suited for Burpees and Burbanks!

If you are finally able to get a coconut palm to germinate, its care and feeding will require the most painstaking attention of the deepest green thumbs. Never cut off a portion of a growing palm! This may be an exotic tree, but it doesn't thrive on the abuse which appeals to mangoes and loquats. However, go ahead and remove the lower dead leaves as they yellow and begin to drop from the growing tree.

If the fronds get dusty, wash them with warm water as you support them with your other hand. A sponge bath is best done in the early morning. Never let the plant dry in bright sunlight—one reason to avoid afternoon baths.

A palm tree will always need high temperatures and bright light if it's going to be both healthy and happy. An indoor temperature of 80° is ideal, although it will grow in lower temperatures ranging from 72° to 75°. This plant should have the sunniest exposure possible, preferably in the direct light of a south window. Avoid chills and cold drafts (from frosted windows and open doors in the winter).

Palms grow naturally in damp sections of tropical islands where the drainage is good. Keep the soil moist around the plant, allowing the surface to dry out slightly between waterings. The coconut palm is most comfortable in sterilized soil to which sharp sand has been added. A deep clay pot is one of the best growing containers for expanding plants. Excess water will evaporate through the sides of the pot even after a thorough drenching. A large pot allows a healthy root system to form at the base of the plant. If the pot is heavily crocked, these roots should have a good supply of vital air and will never drown in excess water.

Admittedly, the palm is one of the toughest plants to grow indoors. It makes an attractive novelty plant and, when grown from scratch, will provide living proof of your deep-green thumb.

## CROTON

Over 100 varieties of croton were originally found from the Fiji Islands to Australia. This is an exotic and colorful foliage plant with thick stems and large, leathery leaves. Colors of the leaves range from brilliant reds and oranges to light pink. The leaves also come in a variety of unusual shapes—some are long and narrow while others are wide and wrinkled. This is a stunning plant grown mainly for its multicolored foliage.

The croton is one of the most demanding indoor plants, really suited to tropical conditions. It is generally grown in a large pot since it has a heavy root system which supports foliage 3 to 10 feet tall. Croton is a high-humidity plant—set the pot on a saucer filled with pebbles and water. The water should not touch the bottom of the pot, or it will cause root rot. Mist the plant occasionally in the winter, moving it out of bright light when you mist. To survive in an apartment, the croton should be placed in the brightest light possible, ideally exposed to the brilliant sun in a south window. Let the soil dry out slightly between waterings. Water heavily enough so that water pours out of the bottom drainage holes.

The croton requires fertilizing once a month from early spring to late fall, which is its active growing period. During the winter months, limit feedings to once every 6 to 8 weeks.

In the average apartment it is easy to provide high temperatures in which the croton thrives. Ideally, it should be 70° to 80° in the day and about 62° to 70° at night. Drafts and quick dips in temperature are disastrous, causing the brilliant leaves to fall off.

You can prune croton plants. The best time to do this is in the spring or early summer. The slips or cuttings from the growing tips can be rooted in moist sand. Cuttings should have mature wood at the base. Cut just below one of the budded joints and remove the leaves. Dip the base of the cutting in a rooting hormone. To get a cutting to root requires a temperature of 80° and high humidity. You can supply bottom heat to the pot with heating cables and cover the plant and pot with a plastic bag to keep the humidity high around the cutting. Keep the soil moist at all times. Check it daily by lifting the plastic bag. Opening the bag also allows fresh air to circulate around the plant. Roots should begin to form at the base of the wood within 6 to 12 weeks. Once a healthy root system has developed, pot the croton in a 6-inch pot containing sterilized soil. Leaves in young plants are green, but will develop color later. A warning: when working with the croton, you'll notice that it exudes a white sap. This sap can irritate your skin, so you should wear gloves or wash your hands immediately after handling the plant.

Another method of getting a young plant from a parent is to support the main stem with a long piece of bamboo. Then make a deep cut about 12 inches from the growing tip under a node from which a leaf grew. Make sure that the cut is below any growing foliage. The cut should slant upwards and slice one third of the way into the stem. Be careful when you're doing this to support the stem so that it doesn't snap off with the pressure of the knife. Insert a wooden matchstick or several pieces of toothpicks into the wound to keep it open and dust with rooting hormone.

Cover the wound and surrounding stem with a handful of moist sphagnum moss (let it soak in warm water for an hour). Tie a piece of plastic about 10 inches square around the moss to keep it in place. The string at the bottom and top of the plastic should be tight enough to keep the moss secured to the stem. Open the top string each week to check on the dampness of the moss. If it's beginning to dry out, mist it until it's thoroughly moist. Tie the plastic back in place. Roots should begin to form within 2 months. As soon as the moss is filled with growing roots sprouting from the wound, cut the stem below the moss with a sharp knife and plant the top portion of the croton in sterilized soil. This process, known as "air layering," is the best way to reduce the size of a plant which has outgrown its allocated space. As with cuttings, the best time to air-layer a croton is in the spring or early summer. (See page 108 for illustration.) Please note that the parent plant from which you take this cutting will likely sprout new growth, so don't toss it away!

Crotons can also be grown from seed supplied by exotic-seed companies. It's a long process, but it does have one advantage—the seedlings will be accustomed to the conditions in your apartment. As with all plants, the young can adapt much more readily to poor growing conditions than the mature plants you buy in the florist shop. In fact, many growers find that crotons lose many of their leaves if purchased in a florist shop and brought into the poorer light conditions of an apartment.

This exotic and colorful plant is a tough one to grow indoors. Yet for the deep-green thumb it will provide stunning foliage year round if cared for properly.

## DATE PALM

When traveling through southern Europe, you'll see
scattered date palms with orange clusters of fruit underneath the lovely feathery branches. However, the climate
is neither dry nor warm enough for these dates to mature
properly; they are used as feed for livestock. In northern
Africa, though, you'll find many regions where date trees
produce edible fruit. Egypt produces many of the world's
finest dates.

According to legend, the date palm was created from
the same clay as Adam. Nomadic tribes refer to the date
palm as the "Tree of Life." Its mystical importance to
them is understandable, since it is a symbol of the life
force in an arid land. In most religions the date palm has
been a symbol of fertility and eternal life. Date palms
usually grow near an oasis and supply rich food which
can be stored and dried for long trips.

The dates which you find in most grocery stores have
been pasteurized. This process not only retards the
growth of mildew and mold, but inhibits the seeds in the
dates from growing. Many health food stores stock natural dates which have not been pasteurized.* These dates
are generally displayed in large plastic bins. Many times
different varieties of dates are available. Why not sample
some of each? You'll find that dates are quite inexpensive. Naturally, each date holds a seed which is a potential palm.

Dates, really one-seeded berries, have dark-brown
wrinkled skin. They're usually about 1 inch long and
½ inch wide. Ripe fruit tends to be mushy and somewhat pasty. The sticky pulp has a taste reminiscent of
fresh acorn squash. Fresh dates are packed with natural

---

* You can purchase date seeds from J. L. Hudson Seedsman,
P.O. Box 1058, Redwood City, California 94064. Seeds are
usually shipped in the fall.

sugar, making them a popular health food. They're often used in cakes, candies, and pastries, or you can eat them right out of the bin. You don't have to cook or dry them to enjoy their rich taste.

After eating the dates, save the seeds for your indoor garden. Each seed is almost as long as the date itself. The deep-brown or light-tan seeds have long thin grooves running down the middle like a smile. Each seed is pointed at the end and looks a little like a peanut.

Wash these seeds in warm water to remove any pulp clinging to them. Each seed is covered with a tiny clear sack. Peel this off. File the midsection of the seed to remove a fraction of the outer coating so that the seed can absorb water more easily, or sand off part of the coating with sandpaper. If you're afraid you'll destroy the seeds by doing this, experiment. File some of the seeds and leave others alone. At this point you have a choice in how you want to get the seeds to grow:

(1) You can soak the seeds in an opaque jar containing 1/8 inch warm water. The seeds, placed crack up, should be surrounded by but not fully covered with water. Change the water every 2 or 3 days. When new growth from the seed is about 1/2 inch long, plant the seed lengthwise in a 4-inch pot. The seed should be planted about 1/2 inch deep in loose, airy sterilized potting soil. Extra peat or vermiculite added to a standard potting mixture makes a good growing medium. Potting mixtures are sold in most retail florist shops.

(2) In the second method (the one I prefer), soak the seeds for 1 day in warm water. Plant them 1 inch apart in a large pot. Mist the soil until it is thoroughly moist. Try to keep the soil at a temperature of 80° to 85° by placing the pot on a heating pad, heating coil, or a metal tray resting on the top of a radiator. Although this high temperature is ideal, dates will grow as long as the tem-

perature doesn't dip below 70°. As the dates begin to sprout, gradually move them into bright light. When the seedlings are several inches high, transplant them into 10-inch pots.

(3) You can also grow dates by soaking the seeds over-night before placing them in moist cheesecloth. Try to keep this cheesecloth moist and warm by placing it in a jar which will act as a miniature greenhouse. Open the jar every 3 days to allow fresh air in. When the dates begin to sprout and root growth reaches ¼ inch, trans-plant the seeds into individual 4-inch pots.

All of these methods are most successful when tem-peratures are high. Neither the soil nor the cheesecloth should dry out around germinating seeds, but neither should it be soggy. Once a plant is in its own pot, place it in a sunny spot (a southern exposure is best). Young plants need moist soil to survive. As they take root and begin to grow well, you can let the surface of the soil dry out between waterings. Don't prune date palms. The palm has only one growing tip—don't cut it! Dates adore dry, hot, sunny corners of apartments and houses. When your young date palm seems to be outgrowing its small home, repot it in a 10-inch pot. This should be a good home for several years. Frost is the only enemy of the date palm. Never let the plant get chilled or caught in a cold draft. Move it away from any frigid window in the winter.

Date palms with their long arching leaves grow 60 to 80 feet high in the wild. Productive trees produce as much as 100 to 200 pounds of dates each year. Indoors, date palms make attractive house plants with a lovely feathery foliage. With central heating it's now possible for dedicated indoor gardeners to grow this exotic plant from the pit of the fruit.

# FERNS

Three hundred million years ago ferns were the dominant life form on this planet. Much of the earth's surface was covered with these gorgeous and unusual plants which reached the height of 100 feet or more. Today, there are still as many as 12,000 different species of ferns. Some of them can live only in the shadow of giant waterfalls where the humidity is a constant 100 percent. Others are far less demanding, but all ferns are moisture-loving plants.

Without moisture, ferns would not be able to reproduce in their unusual way—with spores instead of seeds. The process of growing ferns from spores is one of the most exciting challenges for the deep-green thumb. It will take as long as 2 years to produce mature plants from the dustlike spores, but many gardeners consider this the ultimate thrill in starting from scratch. Not all ferns produce spores, but most of them do, so you'll be able to create a wide variety of different ferns in this way.

Spores are contained in brown spots known as *sori* on the underside of the tiny leaflets (*pinnae*) which comprise a single frond. These brownish dots form intricate patterns on the leaflets and are sometimes mistaken for minute insects. However, the pattern of the dots is regular and predictable in a way that can not be duplicated by roving pests.

The fern spores are ready to be harvested when the dots turn dark brown or black. Remove the leaflets from the fern and cut them into small pieces. Place ten or twelve of these pieces in a clear envelope. After several days the *sori* or spore cases should burst open, spewing the spores into the envelope. The spores will look like fine dust or powder at the bottom of the envelope.

When the spores are ready to be planted, prepare several pots in the following way. Fill three or more 5-inch clay pots with broken crock or pebbles. Use new

1
2

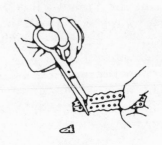

Fern spores are ready to be harvested when the tiny dots on the underside of a frond turn dark brown or black. Cut off several of the leaflets.

Cut the leaflets into small pieces.

3
4

Place ten or twelve of these pieces in a clear envelope for several days. During this time the spore cases will burst open. The spores will collect at the bottom of the envelope and look like a fine dust.

Prepare a growing medium by baking moist peat in a 4-inch casserole for 3 hours at 350° F.

5

6

Fill three or more *new* 5-inch pots halfway full with sterile crocking.

Fill the pots with sterilized peat, leaving a ¾-inch space at the top of each pot. Pack the peat firmly into the pot with your fingers.

7

8

Flatten the surface of the peat by pushing a second pot into the growing medium. Be sure that the hole in the second pot has been covered with strapping tape.

Sift sterilized peat moss through a sieve or 1/16-inch screen until the entire surface is covered with a fine layer. Mist the peat until it's thoroughly moist.

9

10

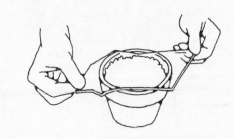

Gently tap the clear plastic envelope containing the spores until the fine dust reaches the opening. Tap the packet lightly while moving your hand back and forth gently over the surface of the peat. Keep your hand about 3 inches above the peat.

Cover each pot with clear glass, leaving a tiny gap between the glass and the pot for air circulation.

11

12

Keep the surface of the peat moist and warm at all times. In less than 3 months tiny heart-shaped plants with miniature roots should appear. Give these plants bright indirect light and very moist growing conditions.

Within four months young ferns should begin to form. Give them 15 hours of daily light. Once they have several leaves, transplant them into sterilized soil, using a tweezers.

pots and be sure that the crocking is sterile by washing it well and pouring boiling water over it. Ideally, you should break up a new clay pot and use it for crocking. Fill the pots halfway with the broken crock or pebbles. Wash your hands carefully and pour boiling water over the pot and crocking. Also, soak them for 5 minutes in a solution of nine parts water to one part Clorox to kill germs. Rinse off any trace of Clorox with warm water. If this seems absurd, remember that many spores are cultivated by professionals in petri dishes which are completely free of germs.

At this point you should prepare a light soil mixture for the spores by rubbing peat moss through a fine screen or sieve. You're going to be working with minute spores, so the growing medium must be extra fine. Pour the peat into a large glass casserole or cake pan (no deeper than 4 inches) and add some water to it. Bake the peat for 3 hours at a temperature of 350°.

Once again, wash your hands carefully. When the peat is cool, moisten it with a mister until it's thoroughly damp. Fill the pots with the peat, leaving about ¾ inch of space at the top of each pot. Pack the peat with your fingers until it's nearly level. Use the bottom of another *sterile* pot to push down on the peat surface to get rid of any possible air pockets where mold is likely to develop. Cover the hole of the other pot with strapping tape or you'll end up with a tiny mound of peat sticking up from the surface. Over this level surface, sift sterilized peat moss through a $\frac{1}{16}$-inch screen or sieve, covering the soil with a fine and very thin layer of peat. Mist the peat until it's thoroughly moist.

After all this work you're ready to plant the spores. You'll discover that these spores are practically impossible to see as you spread them on the soil. A frond can actually produce several million spores. To scatter them evenly across the entire soil surface you must be in a room where there is no breeze. Spores float in drafts, even slight ones, so find an absolutely calm spot to work in.

To plant the spores, open the clear plastic envelope and gently tap it until the dust begins to appear at the opening. If the angle is right, you'll be able to tap the packet lightly while moving it back and forth gently over the surface of the soil. Your hand should be about 3 inches above the soil surface. Tap the packet and move your hand back and forth in a pendulum motion as the spores float down to the soil surface. Don't expect to see the spores on the dark peat moss.

Cover each of the pots with a sheet of clear glass or plastic which will keep the humidity high and allow the surface of the soil to retain moisture. Leave a tiny gap between the plastic and the pot so some air can circulate. Check the peat frequently; if it's drying out, mist as gently as possible. The pots should be in a warm room with indirect light.

In less than 3 months you should see the formation of a tiny, flat, green heart-shaped plate with miniature roots. When a number of these appear, move the pots into bright light without direct sunshine. Keep the surface of the soil moist—almost glistening—but not soggy. This will help the sex cells of the small plants (*prothallus*) unite to create a fern. Under ideal conditions young fern plants begin to form within 2 to 4 months. They need 15 hours of daily light at this time. Fluorescent lights are fine and should be placed 6 inches over the plants. The plants can be transplanted into sterile soil when they've formed several leaves. You can transplant them quite easily by holding the leaf with a pair of tweezers and lifting the soil underneath with a pencil or tongue depressor. Plants should be spaced about 1/2 inch apart in the early stage of their growth. Maintain high humidity at all times. An aquarium converted into a makeshift greenhouse is an ideal spot to grow young ferns. They can remain in this spot for up to a year before being transplanted to individual pots. You'll have an adult fern in 2 years.

The secret to growing ferns from spores is cleanliness, high humidity, warmth, and lots of patience. More conventional growing techniques are usually chosen to obtain quicker results. As a matter of fact, you'll have to try something different with a Boston fern, since it doesn't even produce spores.*

Instead, the Boston fern produces thin threads which extend from its base. Don't cut these off, because they're all potential plants. Fill a 3- or 4-inch pot with sterile soil and place it next to the adult plant. Stick the end of the runner into the soil and water it until thoroughly moist. If the runner will not stay in place, use a bobby pin to peg it down. Keep the soil moist until 2 or 3 tiny fronds appear from the soil. Cut the newly growing plant from its parent.

You can also divide large Boston and maidenhair ferns by pulling the clumps of roots and fronds apart with your hands. Water the plants several hours before making the separation. Knock the plant out of the pot and pull the root system apart, trying to make an even division of the clump so that fronds and roots are still attached. Sometimes you'll have to use a sharp knife to do this. Pot the new sections immediately in smaller pots and soak thoroughly. Keep the new plants covered in a plastic bag for high humidity. Leave them in the bag and don't let the soil dry out around them until the ferns seem to recover from the surgery. Once they're growing again, poke a few holes in the bag to allow a little more air to circulate. When the ferns look more rigid the bag can be removed. Frankly, division is not recommended.

In dry and well-heated modern apartments and houses,

---

* Apartment-grown Boston ferns won't produce spores, although large specimens in conservatories and in the ideal conditions of Florida will.

ferns are difficult to take care of. However, if you're conscious of the plants' needs, you should be able to keep
them healthy and attractive. Grow ferns in a cool, bright
location. Both north and east windows make ideal spots.
A southern exposure is fine as long as the sun's rays
are filtered by a curtain. Avoid drafts and keep the temperature at about 70° in the day and 60° to 65° at night.

The real problem in growing ferns indoors is the lack
of humidity. Ferns thrive in moist soil and humid air.
Try to keep the soil moist at all times. If it begins to dry
out, give the plant a thorough watering. Every 2 or 3
weeks give the fern a foliage bath by dunking it in warm
water. This will also help to prevent scale, mealy bugs,
and red spider mites. Misting is equally helpful to provide
high humidity around the plant. Always mist a fern out
of direct light. Let it dry before placing it in bright light
again. Grouped together, ferns look lovely in any room.
You may want to place the pots in a tray filled with
pebbles and water. To keep the humidity high, never
allow the water to touch the bottoms of the pots, which
will cause root rot.

Ferns need to be fertilized frequently—no matter what
some books or florists say! Do this once a month; you'll
get healthier and greener plants as a result. Ferns do well
in cramped quarters, and can often stay in the same pot
for several years. Only repot when it seems absolutely
essential and go up no more than 1 inch in size.

Ferns make lovely house plants once you realize that
they're quite demanding. With the trend toward lower
winter temperatures, they have a good chance of making
a popular comeback. Supply them with enough humidity,
and you'll find a rich green reward in their graceful and
flowing beauty.

# FIG

Drawings of fig trees date back to 4200 B.C., indicating that the fig was among the first fruit trees to be cultivated by ancient man. Although classified as a subtropical tree, the fig has been able to survive in a remarkable range of climates including that of the east coast where George Washington grew fig trees in his garden at Mt. Vernon. Admittedly, the majority of figs seen on the grocer's shelf (usually from May to September) have been shipped in from the warmest corners of California.

Figs are extremely fragile fruits which should be eaten as soon as they're ripe. The color of a ripe fig varies according to its variety and ranges from greenish yellow and orange to reddish brown and black. The color is not important, though. You should choose this fruit by squeezing it gently in your palm. Ripe figs will be on the firm side but give slightly with a light squeeze. Those which are soft or a bit mushy are not good to eat, although the indoor gardener can easily use the seeds to grow fig trees. The pulpy flesh, used as the center of Fig Newtons, is often served with orange liqueur and whipped cream.

To get to this flesh, peel the fig beginning at the stem and pulling the outer skin off in strips. The pulp inside is delicious and rich in vitamins A and C. Well protected in the inner part of the fruit are many seeds, which you should remove from the flesh and wash until they're completely free of pulp.

Some of these seeds are fertile while others will never germinate. To separate those which are viable, dump all the seeds into a glass of water. The fertile seeds will sink to the bottom while the infertile ones float. Plant only the seeds which remain on the bottom of the glass. (Don't be shocked to find some figs with no fertile seeds—store-bought figs are often infertile.)

Moist vermiculite, perlite, or peat moss makes a good

growing medium for the small seeds. Cover the seeds lightly in a flat or dish filled with any of these. Keep the seeds as warm as possible in indirect light, never allowing the soil to dry out. To keep the humidity high, cover the flat with plastic or a piece of glass. Germination is erratic so don't give up even if it takes weeks or months to see sprouts. Just keep the soil continually moist and warm.

When the seedlings begin to emerge through the soil, move the flat into brighter light. Do this gradually, allowing the plantlets to get used to the sun. Treat them as you would treat yourself in the beginning of the summer before you've gotten a tan. Remove the plastic or glass covering, allowing air to circulate freely around the seedlings, but continue to keep the soil moist.

When the plants are several inches high, move them into individual pots. Give them a good soaking and keep them out of bright light until they recover from the transplanting. Then gradually move them into the warmest spot in your apartment with plenty of sunshine. Figs like to be misted, and you'll want to wash the leaves with lukewarm water to keep them clean. Repot the plant each fall adding new soil. When you repot a plant, you may want to prune it slightly to give it an attractive shape. Pruning does not hurt healthy fig trees. It's a good idea to wear gloves when pruning, since many people are allergic to the fig tree's sap. Don't worry if your tree loses leaves in the fall and stays bare for several months in the winter. The tree does have a dormant period. During this dormant period water the plant *very lightly*. You can also let the temperature drop drastically by setting the pot in one of the coolest spots in the house, since you'll want to use the warmest winter location for other exotic plants. In late February bring the fig tree back into a warm location with as much sun as possible and give it a good soaking. This will bring it back to life.

Although figs grow as high as 30 feet in subtropical

regions, you'll have a dwarf variety in your apartment. Small pots or tubs restrict root growth and inhibit the tree from reaching for the ceiling. The fig tree has the strange habit of forming flowers within the fruit itself, and these flowers can only be pollinated by a unique wasp which pushes its way into the fruit. Since fruit will rarely grow on indoor plants, you'll have to settle for a foliage plant, a unique one which takes tremendous patience and skill to grow from seed.

## GINGER

The Chinese people season many of their most appetizing dishes with a light touch of ginger, a tuberous root (rhizome) that grows in tropical areas. Ginger plants grow about 3 to 4 feet high with dark glossy green leaves. Their lovely scented flowers are used by Hawaiians for making leis. The colors of the flowers vary from deep red to yellow and white.

Throughout much of the year you'll find ginger in specialty produce departments or in fruit markets. Groups of three or more rhizomes are sold in packages tightly sealed with clear plastic. These rhizomes look like a tan root with a number of bumps on it and come in a fanciful variety of unusual shapes. The little bumps indicate fresh growth and are the best part for cooking. Each of these roots can become a lush ginger plant if treated properly.

Try to pick firm rhizomes which don't feel mushy between your fingers. Soft rhizomes are unlikely to grow. Place a root so that part of it is touching water. You can use toothpicks to support the rhizome above water as you would with avocados and yams. Stick several tooth-

# GINGER

**1**

**2**

Stick several toothpicks into a firm ginger root so that its base can rest in a glass filled with water.

Part of the root should begin to swell and turn light green within several weeks. Small roots also emerge at the base of the bump. Cut this bump off with about ¾ inch of the parent plant.

**3**

**4**

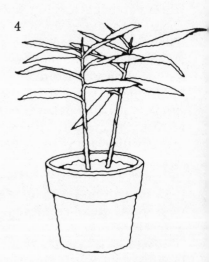

Plant the tiny bump in a pot filled with sterilized soil.

Keep it moist and warm so that it will sprout into a mature ginger plant with its characteristic scent.

picks into the firm flesh and rest them on the edge of the glass. Some of the rhizomes are large enough to support themselves on the rim of the glass or bottle. Change the water two or three times a week so that it won't go stale and try to keep the water level the same at all times.

Ginger roots have a tendency to rot. However, if you notice that part of the root (usually one of the small bumps) turns light green or begins to sprout roots, cut this bump off along with about ½ to ¾ inch of the parent plant. Do this with a sharp razor blade making sure not to include any rotting pulp. This tiny bump should be planted ½ inch deep in moist vermiculite, peat moss, or sterilized soil. Unfortunately, some ginger roots have been boiled to inhibit growth. For these you'll need patience until they sprout.

You can also plant ginger roots or rhizomes directly in soil. Lay the roots 1 inch deep, horizontally, in a large pot filled with sterilized soil. Saturate the soil until it's completely moist. Ginger adores high temperatures between 70° and 80° and should be kept moist at all times. With luck the ginger will begin to sprout within 10 days, but don't be discouraged if it takes 2 or 3 months. Sometimes, the ginger root has to be revived after its long period of drought from being on the grocer's shelf. If the root begins to rot in the soil, dig it up and remove all but the firm spots. Plant these in fresh soil. They may still sprout. Be patient! Whether you plant the root in water or directly in soil, place the plant in a sunny location as soon as you see active shoots rising from the root. A bright east window is great.

You don't need to mist this plant. The moisture in the soil will keep it growing vigorously. As long as you keep the plant in a bright location, it will grow well. However, in late fall you may notice that the leaves turn yellow and begin to die. This is natural, and you're not doing anything wrong. If this should take place, cut down on the watering and finally stop it altogether. Snip off the dead leaves and place the pot in a cool, dark spot until February. In late February, water the seemingly dead plant. Keep the soil moist but not soggy until new growth begins to emerge once again. Treat the "new" ginger plant as you did the old one with lots of warmth and plenty of sunshine.

With luck, you'll have the plant flower sometime in the summer, filling your apartment with its sweet scent. Even if this never happens, you'll appreciate ginger for its lovely green foliage, which when snipped or crushed exudes a fantastic fragrance.

## GUAVA

The guava, a fruit well known to the Aztecs, grows 30 feet high in tropical regions. Today, guava is commercially cultivated in Hawaii, Florida, and southern California, where the hot and dry climates suit it perfectly. The fruit, rich in vitamins A and C, has a flavor somewhat similar to pineapple and strawberries. It's generally available from September to December. You can make delicious juice, jam, and jellies from it.

The guava is shaped like a small lemon and is either green or yellow depending upon the variety. A few rare guavas from Brazil are a purplish red color. The unusual odor of this exotic fruit is one of its most distinctive characteristics. As with most tropical and subtropical fruit, the guava has a disagreeable taste unless it's fully ripe.

To choose a ripe fruit, give the guava a light squeeze in the palm of your hand. It should give slightly to this pressure. If it doesn't give easily and is hard, it's still immature and inedible. Once you've found a ripe fruit, wash it well at home. Remove the stem, the hard ends of the fruit, and any blemishes on the skin. You can peel off the waxy skin or leave it on depending upon personal taste. The yellow pulp surrounds a creamy white layer that is both juicy and full of small, hard seeds.

To remove the pulp from the seeds push the fruit through a sieve after slicing it into thin layers. The flavor of this juicy mush is unusual and quite sharp. Many people like it mixed with fruit drinks or as a topping to a fruit-flavored sherbet.

Don't toss the seeds away! You now have the chance of growing them into small guava trees. Wash the seeds in tepid water and let them dry on a newspaper overnight. Plant them about $\frac{1}{16}$ inch deep in sterilized soil. Mist the soil until it's thoroughly moist and keep it as warm as possible in indirect light. If you place a piece of plastic or a pane of glass over the flat or pot, you'll keep the humidity high, which encourages quick growth. Be sure to remove the cover each day to allow fresh air in. Often, guava seeds will germinate in 2 to 3 weeks, but don't give up if it takes longer. Just keep them continually moist and warm.

When the seeds begin to sprout, take off the glass cover to allow air to circulate around the plantlets. Move the flat into bright light. Continue to keep the soil warm and *slightly* moist. As soon as the seedlings are 1½ inches high, transplant them into individual pots. Give them a good soaking, but once they take root and are growing well, you can allow the soil to dry out for 1 or 2 days between waterings. With lots of heat, bright light, and relatively dry surroundings, the guava should be about 1 foot high in 16 months.

To avoid frequent repotting you can transplant the guava into a large pot or tub. If you use a tub, be sure to bore drainage holes in the bottom to prevent root rot. Set the pot or tub on a large saucer filled with rocks, marbles, or coarse sand so that any water escaping from the bottom of the tub can evaporate quickly. The guava appreciates heavy, infrequent waterings. After a good soaking, water will always pour out of the bottom of a pot or tub. Naturally, you must water this tree more heavily in late spring and summer than in the winter. Fertilize the plant during its active growing season. It doesn't need misting, although you should wipe the dust and grime from its leaves whenever you think of it.

You won't hurt the guava tree by pruning it into any shape you like. Most growers suggest that light pruning should be done when the plant is in dormancy. March is a good month. New growth will appear in the spring and early summer.

Some fortunate indoor gardeners will be rewarded with small white flowers on this attractive tree, but most deep-green thumbs will have to settle for a small bush covered with delightful red-veined green leaves.

## KIWI FRUIT *(Chinese gooseberry)*

Kiwi fruit is native to China where it develops on vines that grow wild along the edges of forests in the Yangtze Valley. About seventy years ago it was imported to New Zealand. Now, 1800 acres of northern New Zealand are devoted to the commercial growing of this exotic fruit. Although kiwi fruit is now being planted in select parts of California, it will be some time before the Californian fruit compares in size and taste to those grown in New Zealand.

Kiwi fruit appears infrequently on the shelves of grocery stores. Since the demand for this unusual fruit is not yet high, grocers tend to import it only as a novelty item for a few selective or inquisitive customers. The fruit looks like a large egg covered with a tan fuzz. The outer coating just underneath this "five o'clock shadow" is tannish green. The green color disappears as the fruit becomes fully ripe.

Although you can buy kiwi fruit when it's still immature, you won't want to eat it until it's somewhat soft to the touch. Unripe fruit will be firm to the touch and quite flavorless. The indoor gardener should not try to grow plants from the seeds of unripened fruit since they will not sprout! If you're not familiar with kiwi fruit, ask the grocer to show you some in different stages of maturity. A mature kiwi fruit has about the same feel as a ripe pear.

To get to the delicious core of this rather ugly fruit, simply cut off the outer coating with a sharp knife. The light green pulp adds a special touch to sherbets and cold drinks. When peeled in this way, kiwi fruit looks like a miniature melon and has just about as many seeds. Hundreds of tiny dark brown seeds are tucked into pale green pouches which border the white central vein.

You will need a good sense of humor as you begin to separate these miniscule seeds from the pulp. One semi-efficient way of doing this is to cut the fruit like a cucumber into six or seven thin slices. Squeeze the seeds between your thumb and forefinger to pop them out of the pulp. You can gather them into one spot by pushing them together with the fingernail of your thumb. This is a messy job, best done over a piece of absorbent paper.

Try to collect seeds from all parts of the fruit. By the time you're done you'll have a number of seed-filled pieces of pulp. Float these in a warm glass of water and swish them around until some of the pulp washes free. Then, take a washcloth, place it over an empty glass, and pour the water and seeds onto it. The water flows through the cloth into the glass leaving behind some pulp and all the seeds. Stretch the cloth out on a hard surface and rub the seeds in circles until you've separated them completely from any pulp. The pulp clings to the cloth while the seeds move freely.

Now you'll have to pretend that you're Mother Nature. Since kiwi fruit grows in a temperate climate, it does lose its leaves before going through a cool season of several months. You'll have to trick the seeds into believing that they've had their winter's rest. So, dry the seeds overnight, place them in a plastic bag filled with moist peat moss, and tuck them into a corner of the refrigerator. Technically, the seeds should be kept at a temperature of 41° for 2 weeks. After this initial winter stage, they should be shocked with changing temperatures varying from 50° at night to 68° in the day for 2 to 3 weeks. Since most of us are not that technical, we leave the seeds in the refrigerator at about 45° for 5 weeks. Two or three sprouting seeds will be enough.

Once "winter" is over for the kiwi seeds, they can be planted in 2½-inch pots or in a flat from which they'll be transplanted as seedlings. Seeds of the kiwi fruit are so small that you should cover them very lightly with no more than ⅛ inch of soil, or simply press the seeds into the soil with your finger so that they're barely covered. Mist the soil frequently so that it's always moist, but never soggy. Seeds should begin to sprout in 2 to 8 weeks. As with all unusual fruit seeds, don't give up too soon. They can be very stubborn.

If you've started seeds in a flat, be extremely careful as you transplant them. Don't transplant until the seedlings are firmly rooted and 1 to 2 inches high. They should have 4 leaves at that time. Moisten the soil several hours before transplanting. To avoid root damage, you should take as much soil as possible with the plant when placing it in a pot, which measures 4 to 6 inches in depth.

Kiwi fruit vines like a humid atmosphere. The soil around the roots should be moist. Place the plants in a sunny location where they'll grow best. The fuzzy, heart-shaped leaves have a distinctive silver tinge. The vine should have support, allowing it to curl upward as it would in the wild. As the vine grows, remove any dead leaves at its base. You may want to dust the plant occasionally with a soft camel's-hair brush, but don't mist the leaves as you would with most other plants.

If you have a friend who would like a kiwi fruit plant, you can snip off a 6-inch portion of a half-ripened stem at the tip of the vine. Dip the end in *Rootone* and place it 1 to 2 inches deep in moist sand. Keep the plant warm without letting the sand dry out even for a day. The vine should root in sterile sand after 6 to 8 weeks.

In late fall and early winter your plant may go into a dormant state. At this time it will lose its leaves and stop growing. Cut the vine back to one-third of its original length. Water only once a month while the plant takes a siesta. When the plant begins to grow again, resume watering as usual. You may have to give the plant a push. If it doesn't show signs of growth by late April or early May, begin to water as usual. The vine should come back to life.

The ornamental kiwi fruit vine is a striking house plant. In the wild it grows to a length of 30 feet and blossoms with lovely creamy white flowers. Indoors, this rarely occurs. However, the striking foliage of the kiwi fruit is ample reward for the ardent gardener seeking the unusual and unique for his indoor jungle.

## LITCHEE *(also Lychee or Litchi)*

For over 2000 years the Chinese have been cultivating the evergreen litchee tree for its highly prized fruit. The trees are covered with long, thin leaves that seem almost leathery and shiny. The leaves change from an orange-copper color when young to an unusual shade of green when older. Trees grown along canals, ponds, and rice paddies reach the height of 35 to 40 feet and have been known to live as long as 8 centuries.

This exotic fruit is available only in the summer, generally from late May until early August. The best time to find it in specialty stores is in the second or third week of June. Sometimes, litchee is served as a dessert in Polynesian or Oriental restaurants. However, it's a rare fruit, and you may have to order it unless you live in cities with a large Chinese community, where the fruits are relatively common.

Litchees are small grape-size fruits, about 1½ inches long. Some are light green while most are a rosy red. The fruit is covered with a knobby, rough shell which is easily broken to reveal a juicy, white pulp. The pulp has a distinctive fragrance, almost like the perfume from a flower. The delectable taste more than makes up for its high cost.

Litchees are very perishable. They have to be flown in from the subtropical areas where they're grown. Choose fruit that is firm with no sign of bruises or rot. The seeds inside the fruit are also very delicate. They generally survive for 3 weeks in the fruit and will die within 3 days after being removed from the moist pulp. The secret to growing litchees is to plant the seeds immediately after removing them from the fruit.

Suck out the seeds from the delicious pulp and wash them in warm water. Plant them immediately about ½ inch deep in vermiculite, perlite, and peat moss. Mist the growing medium until it's very moist. Normally, the litchee seeds will begin to sprout within 2 weeks. But don't give up if it takes several weeks longer. Just keep the soil moist and warm at all times. By placing plastic or glass over the growing tray, you'll keep the humidity high around the germinating seeds. Lift the glass daily for air circulation.

The fragile seedlings should be placed in bright light as soon as they emerge through the soil. Remove the plastic or glass cover, but keep the soil very moist—almost soggy. Unfortunately, you'll probably have a high mortality rate with these unusual plants. This is not uncommon. If two or three plantlets survive, consider that good odds. When the seedlings are several inches high, transplant them carefully into a large pot filled with rich soil. Try not to disturb the root system. Always keep the plants in bright light. Mist the foliage as frequently as possible during the dry winter and don't worry if the soil tends to be soggy since these plants will survive as long as there is adequate drainage. Excess water should freely drain into a dish filled with pebbles below the pot. If you keep the dish partially filled with water as well, you'll increase the humidity around the growing tree.

Litchees love hot humid summers and will survive cooler and somewhat dry winters. As the temperature drops in late fall, reduce the watering considerably. The trees can be clipped back and trained to curve around

It's very difficult to find litchees, but slightly less difficult to get the large brown seeds inside to germinate. Litchees like a moist soil and plenty of sunshine. The delicate pink leaves slowly turn green as the plant matures.

windows, but remember to remove the plant from a chilly window in winter.

Commercial growers are familiar with the small white flowers that become the delectable litchee "nut," but most indoor gardeners should be satisfied in getting this finicky seed to grow into a foliage plant. It's a stiff challenge!

## MONSTERA DELICIOSA *(Mexican breadfruit)*

The *Monstera deliciosa* is a jungle vine native to Mexico. It produces a large pine cone-shaped fruit *ceriman* which has a delicious taste and a pineapple aroma. Since this fruit is an irritant when immature, it must be eaten only when fully ripe. *Monstera deliciosa* is often sold under the misleading name "split-leaf philodendron." (*Monstera*s have been confused with philodendrons because the leaves, when young, lack perforations and resemble philodendron leaves.) Another common name, "Swiss cheese plant," gives a vivid image of the large, indented leaves with a deep-green sheen and leathery texture. The holes in the leaves allow the heavy winds of hurricanes to whistle through the plant without damaging it.

Caring for *Monstera* is quite easy since it is a tough and adaptable plant. It can tolerate little light but needs a lot of moisture. Never let the soil dry out. Since it grows best with support, you should tie the stem of the plant to a split log—this is the way the plant is sold in florist shops. Mist the plant often, and when you water or fertilize it, let the liquid pour down the log on its way to the root system. This will moisten the aerial roots clinging to the support. Misting helps keep the plant clean, but from time to time you may want to give it a

You can transform a mature *Monstera deliciosa* into a smaller plant by air layering.

warm shower or sponge off its leaves with warm water. When you sponge the mammoth leaves, be sure to support the base of the leaf with your hand to prevent cracking. Although *Monstera deliciosa* prefers high temperatures, it adapts to temperatures between 65° and 85°.

Getting small plants from *Monstera deliciosa* takes patience, but it's a fascinating process (see page 108 for illustration). Cut off the top growing stem of the plant below the second node from the tip of the plant. The cutting should include one leaf and several aerial roots (the tiny roots clinging to the support) if possible. Place the cutting in a 6-inch pot filled with a mixture of peat moss and perlite. Keep the growing medium constantly moist and place the pot in bright indirect light. Mist it daily and keep the plant covered with a plastic bag. Open the bag each day to allow fresh air to circulate. Within 6 to 12 weeks roots should begin to sprout. When the roots are 6 inches long, repot the plant in a large pot filled with sterilized soil. Continue to keep the plant moist and warm. Use the plastic "tent" until the plant takes root and shows signs of new growth. At that point, remove the tent and treat the new *Monstera deliciosa* as you would a parent plant.

The remaining parent plant will grow new shoots. As a matter of fact, you can cut it all the way back to the first node above the soil. You can then take cuttings from the stem. Each cutting should have two to three nodes. Use a sharp knife and cut the stem about ¼ inch below the node. Place the bottom of the cutting (the part of the stem which was closest to the roots) about 2 to 3 inches into the growing medium in a 6-inch pot. A mixture of peat, vermiculite, and perlite makes an excellent growing medium. Follow the same steps as outlined in the preceding paragraph to keep the temperature and humidity high. The cuttings should take root in about 6 to 12 weeks. This method of starting from scratch will give you many small *Monstera deliciosa* plants.

Growing this plant from seed is a long process, but one that many indoor gardeners find enjoyable. Seed for *Monstera deliciosa* is available from John Brudy's Rare Plant House, P.O. Box 1348, Cocoa Beach, Florida 32931.

The so-called split-leaf philodendron can put up with abuse. If you have a dark corner to fill, why not give this plant a try? But remember, although it tolerates the dark, it prefers bright light from time to time, and it will reward you with luxuriant foliage.

## PASSION FRUIT

The passion fruit is a unique tropical evergreen vine growing from 20 to 30 feet in length. Originally from Brazil, the passion fruit gets its name from its lovely flowers which have become symbolic of the crucifixion. Each part of the fragrant flower is associated in some way with the agony of Christ on the cross. The vine has large leaves and tendrils which cling to supports, to trees in the wild, and to walls or wooden framework in an apartment.

Passion fruit varies from light yellow to deep purple in color. It's either round or oval, generally about the size of a small egg. The rind seems leathery and even hard to the touch. Most people strip off the outer skin and eat the juicy orange pulp with sugar and cream. The pulp is slightly acidic and has an attractive aroma. The most delicious part of the passion fruit is the flesh surrounding the seeds in the central cavity.

Suck the pulp off from around the seeds and then wash them in warm water until they're completely clean. The best time to plant the seeds is in the spring. Seeds should be planted about ¼ inch deep in sterilized soil (which should be moist before planting). Perhaps you'll want to plant a number of seeds in a 6-inch pot. Mist the soil so that it's thoroughly moist. To keep the humidity high around the germinating seeds cover the pot with plastic or a pane of glass. Lift the glass daily to allow for air movement and to check the moisture. The ideal temperature is 78°.

Plants should begin to sprout within 2 to 3 weeks although some seeds may take much longer. When the seedlings are 2 inches tall, you can either thin all but the strongest plant from the pot or transplant the weaker plants to individual 4-inch pots. If you decide to thin the passion fruit seedlings, don't pull them up from the

soil. Cut them with a scissors. This way you won't disturb the root system of the remaining vine.

As the vine grows, try to give it some sort of support.
Either place a stick in the pot or train the vine to cling
to a wall by nailing small tacks into the woodwork. As
the vine becomes larger, it will be necessary to transplant
it into consecutively larger pots until it reaches its permanent home—a tub or pot that's 18 to 24 inches wide. Repotting is best done in February or March.

The passion fruit demands the same care as does a
tropical plant: warmth, plenty of sunshine (a south window is perfect), and loose, rich soil. You can mist the
plant occasionally, but it doesn't need high humidity
to survive.

If the plant is getting out of hand, don't be afraid to
trim it back to a more manageable and attractive length.
The best time to do this is just after the vine finishes
blooming. Remove all of the weak growth and cut the
healthiest part of the plant back by one-third its overall
length.

Your goal in growing this exotic plant is to get it to
flower. If Luther Burbank could create a spineless cactus,
then maybe you too can do the "impossible."

# PERSIMMON

From October to January you may see a bright orange
fruit about the size of a tomato in the exotic fruit section
of some grocery stores. The persimmon, grown in both
tropical and subtropical regions, is known as the "apple
of the Orient." The tree, which grows 40 feet high in
China, has been imported to California where it is cultivated commercially for its fruit.

The most important feature in buying a persimmon is to make sure it's ripe. Immature persimmons have a disagreeable taste while ripe fruit is both rich and sweet. Don't worry about any blemishes on the skin of the fruit. However, you should squeeze a persimmon lightly—the *Hachiya* variety is ripe when it's slightly soft while the *Fuyu* variety is sweet and delicious even when firm. The *Fuyu* variety is slightly flatter in shape than the *Hachiya* variety. Check with the produce manager about the kind he sells.

Peel off the thin skin of the fruit to get to the orange- or salmon-colored pulp. While you're enjoying the delicious flavor of this fruit, be sure to save the seeds for your indoor garden.* Persimmons have from one to ten seeds in each fruit. These flat seeds should be kept for 2 to 3 months in moist vermiculite at a temperature of 50°. Since you buy the fruit in the fall, you can tuck the seeds into a plastic bag partially filled with peat moss and place the bag either in the refrigerator, a cool basement, or on a fire escape where they'll be chilled. After 2 or 3 months of winter, you can plant them about ½ inch deep in sterilized soil. Keep the soil moist and warm. For high humidity cover the pot or flat with plastic or a pane of glass. Lift the pane once a day to allow for air movement.

These seeds are erratic in their germination and can take many weeks and even months to sprout. As long as the soil is warm and damp, you have a good chance of getting several persimmon trees from a full batch of seeds. Once several seeds begin to poke through the surface of the soil, move the pot into bright light and take off the cover. Continue to keep the soil moist and warm.

As soon as the seedlings are 2 or 3 inches high, either thin out the weak plants or transplant them into indi-

* Fruit now found in many supermarkets is seedless—a disappointment for indoor gardeners.

vidual 4-inch pots. With good light, warmth, and adequate water, your persimmon tree should thrive. When it's 2 feet tall, clip off the top inch or two of the plant just above a leaf. This will encourage the plant to branch and will make the stem sturdier.

Persimmon is a lovely ornamental plant with glossy leaves that feel soft underneath—almost downy. You'll lose nothing by trying to start this plant from scratch because the fruit is delicious, and the seeds would only end up in the garbage can otherwise.

## POMEGRANATE

The pomegranate, meaning "seeded apple," was imported from southwestern Asia to England in the sixteenth century. At that time pomegranate trees were grown in heated greenhouses as a novelty plant while today the culture of this unusual fruit tree has spread throughout the world. The tree grows about 15 feet high in the wild with shiny, oblong leaves. In late spring and early summer it blossoms with scarlet flowers. These fertilized flowers produce the exotic fruit found on the grocer's shelf from September through November.

Pomegranates are about the size of a large orange. They are picked from the trees before they're fully ripe. Fortunately, they keep well while being shipped. Pomegranates, varying in color from light yellow to purplish red, have a thick and very tough skin. You'll have to break through this brittle rind to get to the red pulp inside. This pulp, used as a base for grenadine syrup, is considered exquisite by some and rather insipid by others. People in the know about pomegranates insist that the larger varieties have the best-tasting flesh.

The juicy, ruby-red pulp surrounds numerous seeds in the segmented cavities of the fruit, chambered like a large nut. These seeds are small and tender. Although some people discard them, the seeds are delicious. In fact, ancient cultures believed that the pulp and seeds of the pomegranate had a mysterious power to increase fertility.

Assuming that you don't care for the taste or texture of these seeds, you'll want to save them. Each one is a potential pomegranate tree. Wash the seeds in warm water and let them soak for 24 hours. Plant the seeds in sterilized soil about ½ inch deep. Keep the soil moist with frequent mistings; never let it dry out. High temperatures will encourage quick germination. If you cover the pot with plastic or glass, you'll keep the humidity high.

To start a pomegranate tree, wash the pulp and clear sack off each seed before planting. Seedlings may be attacked by damping off, a fungus disease that can destroy an entire batch of plantlets, so be prepared to treat the soil with a proper solution (see p. 195).

Seedlings may begin to appear within 2 weeks, although you should not be discouraged if it takes longer. Once the young trees begin to sprout, move the pot into bright light and remove the plastic cover. Full sun in a south window is a perfect spot for a pomegranate. Continue to keep the soil moist while the plant is still young. When the seedling is several inches tall, move it into its own 4-inch pot.

The pomegranate will continue to thrive in bright light. As soon as the plant is 2 feet high, you should cut off 2 or 3 inches of its growing tip just above a leaf. This will keep it compact and bushy making it a more attractive and healthy plant. If you're interested in the art of bonsai, the pomegranate makes an excellent tree to work with. Whenever the tree seems to be outgrowing its pot, plant it in a larger pot until it's finally in an 18-inch pot or tub which should be large enough for a permanent home. Repotting is best done in spring just as the tree is beginning to show new growth.

Although young pomegranate trees need lots of moisture at all times, larger plants can withstand 2 or 3 days of drying out between waterings. The pomegranate adores fresh air as long as the temperature doesn't drop below 50°. If your apartment doesn't have a south or east window, this compact tree will respond well under fluorescent lights.

The chances of getting a pomegranate tree to flower indoors are better than with many other exotic fruit trees. Still, you should not expect it to bear fruit. It's a versatile, compact, and attractive foliage plant that can be pruned to any shape and size.

## PRICKLY PEAR *(Cactus pear)*

The torrid and desolate island of Lanzarote lies just a short distance west of the Sahara. The land has been known to go without a drop of rain for seven years! Yet one plant is sure to grow—a cactus commonly called prickly pear. Outwardly, these fleshy plants made up of spiny flat leaves or joints seem ugly as they turn light yellow and tan in the grueling sun. Exquisite purple dyes are made from the cochineal insect that feeds on the unusual leaves of this stoic plant. During the late nineteenth century, millions of pounds of dried insects were exported to other nations, including some in the Middle East famous for the color-fast Persian rugs.

Prickly pears also bear an edible fruit which was a favorite with North, Central, and South American Indians. The season for prickly pears in the United States is from September to December and from March to May. During these months you may be able to find prickly pears on the shelves of the produce section in specialty food stores.

The prickly pear is not an attractive fruit. It's about the size of a medium-size potato, and that's where the resemblance ends. Prickly pears have been stripped of all spines before being shipped, but you'll still want to be somewhat careful in picking them up. They have a reddish green or yellow skin. Be sure to choose firm fruit that hasn't shriveled or dried up.

The skin is not edible, and you'll want to slice it off with a sharp knife. Cut the ends of the fruit off first, then slit the fruit lengthwise to pull the skin back. This will reveal a rich pulp, either deep magenta or pineapple-yellow in color. The watermelonlike flesh has a subtle taste. Although popular with the Indians, it takes some getting used to. It's pleasant without being outstanding.

Inside this pulp are dozens of tiny seeds which look

To grow a prickly pear, remove the seeds from a ripe fruit and wash them carefully before drying on a newspaper. Plant the seeds in a sandy growing medium and keep them warm and moist until they germinate. The fleshy seedlings are especially susceptible to damping off, which must be treated with appropriate chemicals (see p. 195).

like miniature match heads. Either suck these from the pulp, pick them individually with your fingers, or push the pulp through a sieve which will leave the seeds behind. The pulp is delicious mixed with cold drinks or spread on ice cream.

Lay the moist seeds on a newspaper after washing them in warm water. You'll have to do this in a pan or glass dish since the seeds can be easily washed down the drain. Let them dry for several days.

Plant the seeds in a one-to-one mixture of sterilized soil and sand. A dish, glass casserole, or flat with drainage holes make good germinating trays. Cover the seeds with about 1/8 inch of sand. Mist the sand until it's thoroughly moist. You can cover the bed with plastic or glass leaving a small opening for air to circulate. This will keep the soil moist. Place the flat in a room where a temperature of 70° is maintained. You can put the seeds in a spot with very little light.

Getting prickly pear seeds to sprout takes time. In the wild, seeds sometimes stay dormant for 20 years. However, you're providing ideal germinating conditions for them. Several of the seeds should sprout within 2 or 3 months, but don't get discouraged. They can take as long as a year to germinate. Needless to say, the growth pattern of these seeds is very erratic.

Once the seedlings emerge from the surface of the sand, move them gradually into bright light. Eventually, they should be growing in a southern exposure with high temperatures and as much sunshine as possible. A lack of light can be corrected by using fluorescent lamps to fool the plant into believing it's in a desert. Reduce watering slightly, letting the surface of the soil go somewhat dry. When the seedlings are several inches high, you can transplant them into individual pots with a soil made up mostly of sand mixed with some sterilized peat and potting mixture.

If seedlings are growing well, water them quite often in late spring and summer. From October to January reduce water considerably and never fertilize in this period. Growing prickly pears from seed is as much a challenge as growing ferns from spores.

A quicker and more effective method of starting from scratch is as follows: sever a leaf or flat joint from an adult plant, preferably in the spring or summer. Allow it to dry for 10 to 14 days to prevent rotting. Place the pad or joint into moist sand. Within several weeks it should be growing roots. Once the plant has taken root, cut down on the watering considerably (soggy sand will cause rot). When a healthy root system has developed, pot the cutting in a one-to-one mixture of sterilized soil and sand.

The needs of the prickly pear are simple and sometimes difficult to meet: bright sun, dry air, and heat.* A prickly pear will grow well, if slowly, for deep-green thumbs who can supply it with all its needs. Within 4 to 5 years you may even get the plant to bloom. Entire hedges of prickly pear covered with radiant red blossoms may be seen in parts of southern Italy.

## REX BEGONIA

The rex begonia is indeed fit for a king. Both its foliage and brilliant flowers are stunning. The large, fuzzy leaves vary from pink and purple to rusty red and silver. The rex begonia grows from 6 to 10 inches tall under the average apartment conditions. Since it has a shallow root system, you may prefer to plant it in an azalea pot (not as deep as a standard pot). Use a light airy soil such as sterilized soil mixed with some peat and vermiculite.

The soil should be kept moist although the foliage should not be misted. If the leaves become dusty, swirl the foliage in warm water and allow it to dry out in a warm and airy room. Don't dry a moist plant by placing it in bright sunlight. The plant does well in temperatures varying from 65° to 75° and in bright *indirect* light. If you prefer to grow the plant with fluorescent lights, leave the light on for 14 to 16 hours a day and place it about 14 inches above the plant. Fertilize the plant during its active growing period, but don't fertilize it while it's flowering.

The rex begonia has a dormant period when the leaves wilt. This is a natural process which takes place

---

* This plant thrives in bright sun, but never place it in direct light of a southern window in the summer. Direct south light from mid-June to the end of August can scorch leaf tissue.

# REX BEGONIA

1

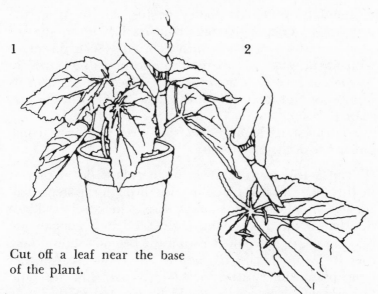

Cut off a leaf near the base
of the plant.

3

Slash the largest veins on the
*underside* of the leaf with a
sharp knife or razor blade.
Cut the veins in several places.

4

Lay the wounded leaf on
moist sterilized sand or vermiculite in a large azalea pot.
Make sure that the *underside*
of the leaf is touching the
sand. Keep the leaf in place
with tiny bits of a broken pot.

As soon as tiny plantlets
emerge from the wounds in
the leaf, they can be planted
in individual pots. Be sure to
get a healthy root system with
each plantlet.

in the fall. When dormancy begins, cut back on the watering and *never* give the plant fertilizer. Store the pot in a cool and airy closet until February. Soak the plant with warm water at this time to encourage new growth. As soon as leaves are growing well, place the plant in its usual spot and treat it with the same TLC as in the preceding season.

You can start rex begonias from seed, but most people prefer one of these methods:

(1) Cut a leaf from the base of the plant (ideal time is in July). Use a razor blade to slice through the stem. The cut leaf should have a stem at least 2 inches long. Place the stem about 1 inch into moist sand in a Forsyth pot (see page 197). The cutting from the begonia should take root in 2 to 4 weeks. As soon as the roots are 4 inches long, plant the cutting in a 4-inch pot. The leaf and any sign of new growth should be planted so that they just touch the surface of the soil. At the base of the stem a new rex begonia will begin to appear. When it is well rooted and has several small leaves, you can cut off the larger leaf with a razor blade. Give the plant lots of warmth and humidity, and very little sun.

(2) Cut off a leaf with a sharp knife or razor blade. Slash the largest veins on the *underside* of the leaf with the razor. Cut the veins in several places. Gently lay the wounded leaf on moist sterilized sand or vermiculite in a pot or flat. Make sure that the base of the leaf is pointing down since the wounds must come in contact with the soil. To keep the leaf in place, put pieces of broken pot or pebbles on the edge. The temperature should be between 70° and 80°; mist the soil whenever it begins to dry out. Within 4 to 6 weeks tiny plantlets will form where the wounds have been made. As soon as the emerging plantlets have several leaves, you can cut them from the parent leaf and plant them in individual 3-inch pots.

(3) Cut off a leaf with a sharp knife or razor blade. From the center of the leaf cut a number of triangles. It's important that each triangle include a portion of the main vein or a large side vein. The vein should run down to the center of the point of the triangle. Insert this point (the end of the vein) about ½ inch deep into moist sand. Keep the soil moist and warm until a plantlet forms at the base of the triangle. As soon as the new plant has several leaves and a good root system, plant it in a 3-inch pot filled with sterilized soil.

You may have some failures with any of these methods, but don't be discouraged. If a leaf rots or wilts without any sign of growth, accept the failure and start over again. The keys to success are warmth, high humidity, and moist sterile sand as a rooting medium.

The rex begonia with its regal appearance is a good plant to work with. It is temperamental, though, especially when you start a new one from scratch. But the resulting plant is worth the time and patience you put into it.

## SCHEFFLERA *(Queensland umbrella tree)*

The schefflera makes an ideal indoor plant. Not only is it tough, but it's also very delicate and beautiful whether it's 2 or 10 feet high. The long shiny leaves fan out like an umbrella from the branching light-green stems. The main trunk turns light tan as the shrub matures. It's a challenging plant to start from scratch, and with proper care it will live for many, many years.

One of the great advantages of starting a schefflera

from scratch is that it's a very expensive plant in florist shops. Furthermore, large plants purchased in a florist shop often are unable to adapt easily to the conditions in your apartment. The loss of such a plant hurts both your pride and your pocketbook. Yet, if you start a schefflera from scratch, the odds are excellent that the plant will survive and thrive in even the poorest environment. Young plants can cope with the kind of abuse that older plants find intolerable.

You can start scheffleras from seed. J. L. Hudson, Seedsman, P.O. Box 1058, Redwood City, California 94064, carries these seeds in stock. If you would like to get a small schefflera from a parent plant, try the following method:

Tie a bamboo stick to the stem of the large plant for support. With a sharp knife make a diagonal cut upwards into the stem, about 12 inches from the terminal bud. The incision should be several inches long and one third of the way through the stem. With several pieces of wooden matchsticks or toothpicks prop the wound open. Dust the wound with rooting hormone. Cover the entire stem and wound with a handful of moist sphagnum moss (let the moss rest in water for an hour until it is damp). Secure the moss in place by wrapping it with a 10-inch-square piece of plastic. Tie the plastic to the stem with two pieces of twine. You should untie the top piece of string once a week to check the moisture of the sphagnum moss. If it begins to dry out, mist it until it's thoroughly moist. (See page 108 for illustration).

Within 6 to 12 weeks roots should begin to form from the wound and spread throughout the moss. When the roots fill the moss area, cut off the top of the plant just underneath the roots. Plant this cutting in a 6-inch pot filled with sterilized soil. Keep the soil moist and warm. To raise the humidity, cover the plant with a plastic bag, but be sure to lift it each day to provide the plant with fresh air. Never place the bag in direct sunlight since it will scorch the leaves. You may keep the plant covered with plastic for a few days, but once the plant seems to be growing well, remove the "tent." Treat the plant at this point just as you did the original parent plant. Never throw away the parent plant, which will recuperate from the operation in time. New growth will take the place of the old decapitated section!

The schefflera is not a demanding or temperamental plant; it's quite adaptable. It prefers bright light, but not the direct glare of the sun in a southern exposure. Set it in an east or west window. Normal apartment temperatures suit it very well. If you can, set the thermostat at 70° in the day with a 10° dip at night at which point both you and your schefflera should be quite comfortable. Let the soil dry out between waterings and give the plant a thorough soaking whenever it's dry.

The waxy leaves of this plant tend to collect dust. Sponge them often with warm water. In between sponge

By air layering mature scheffleras, you'll be able to create healthy new plants.

baths, your schefflera will appreciate thorough mistings on both the bottom and top of the leaves. Since the plant grows rapidly, you may want to cut it back occasionally to encourage branching. Whenever the plant outgrows its pot, move it into a larger pot adding fresh sterilized soil.

A schefflera will be one of your most exciting indoor plants. Radiant and rich in varied greens, it's a most striking shrub. Both its grace and beauty greatly enhance furniture arrangements and decorating schemes.

## SUNFLOWER

Blossoming rows of giant sunflowers with their yellow heads rotating to catch every spark of sunshine are a familiar sight in rural regions of the United States and Canada. The sunflower grows like a weed and its nutritious seeds are a favorite among birds and people as well. Grown indoors, however, it's unlikely to bloom or provide your pet parrot with seed.

With that in mind, you may want to plant the seed indoors as a challenge to see how high it will grow and how close it will come to flower. Why not try one of the dwarf varieties that grow about 3 feet high? These seeds are sold by many seed companies including Northrup King, Minneapolis, Minnesota 55413.

The bushy plants of the dwarf variety will produce attractive blooms under ideal growing conditions of warmth and plenty of sunshine. If your apartment has a

* The sunflower is easy to grow indoors, but it's very difficult to get it to bloom. It takes a deep-green thumb to make it flower.

south window or a fire escape with bright light, you may get this plant to bloom in the summer.

Ideally, you should plant the seeds in late March. They are similar to the salted variety you've eaten but slightly thinner and smaller. Plant these grayish white seeds in a flat or pot about $\frac{1}{2}$ inch deep and about 2 to 3 inches apart. Mist the soil until it's thoroughly moist. Cover the container with plastic or glass to keep the humidity high. Within 3 or 4 days the quick-sprouting seeds will break through the soil. Give them bright light and remove the cover. Keep the soil moist. The young plants grow very quickly. The first two leaves to open up are not true leaves, but the second pair are. As soon as the second pair appears, transplant the seedlings into a large pot. Sunflower seeds are tough and durable so that almost all of them will sprout. It would take 10 or 15 large pots to accommodate all the seedlings which germinate. Perhaps you'll only want to plant 10 or 15 seeds initially. However, if you've planted all the seeds, thin them out during transplanting so that only a few seedlings are allowed to grow in any one pot. Or start several seeds in one 7-inch pot, and remove all but the strongest plant later on. This is the method I prefer since it eliminates any need for transplanting fragile seedlings.

By the end of April or the beginning of May, you should thin the plants to only one to a pot. Since pots are expensive, you may want to use gallon plastic ice cream buckets as containers. Be sure to pierce the bottom of the tubs to provide drainage holes.

Plant care for sunflowers is simple: lots of water, full sun in a south window, and warmth. By the end of May when all danger of frost is past, the plant can be set on a windowsill in fresh air for maximum sun. As a foliage plant, the sunflower is definitely second-rate. But perhaps you'll be surprised with a delightful bright yellow blossom in July or August as a reward for your patience and tender loving care.

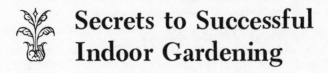

# Chapter V

# Secrets to Successful
# Indoor Gardening

In this chapter you'll find helpful hints for keeping house plants lush and lovely. The suggestions are designed to make you aware of the limitations of the average apartment and house. By following the detailed directions you will develop the greenest of thumbs when working with plants. You'll know how to pot a plant properly, start plants from seed and cuttings, and avoid the most common mistakes that harm or kill house plants. You'll also learn to identify, destroy, and avoid common pests.

Furthermore, you'll discover that indoor gardening does not have to be expensive. Dozens of cost-cutting tips are included in this chapter to keep indoor gardening bills at a minimum.

## HOW TO KEEP THE COSTS DOWN

One of the great advantages of growing your own plants from scratch is that it is so inexpensive. Throughout this guide to indoor gardening you've discovered how easy it is to turn worthless vegetal odds-and-ends into lovely household plants. You've also found out that a friend will provide you with a cutting from a coleus or any other quick-growing plant—all for the asking!

Furthermore, the secret to keeping costs low is to use

common household items in each step of starting a plant from scratch. You don't need a Rube Goldberg set-up to get plants to grow indoors. Here's how to cut those costs:

| Common household items | What to use them for |
|---|---|
| Clear pickle, peanut butter, and mayonnaise jars | Starting pits, germinating seeds, storing seeds |
| Ovaltine, Lipton tea, and other opaque jars | Starting many cuttings in water; storing herbs |
| Egg cartons and plastic ice trays | Use as flats for planting seedlings |
| Glass Windex, Easy-Off bottles, and perfume atomizers | Misters |
| Plastic bread savers, shoe boxes, crisper in refrigerator, enamel vegetable bins, plastic dishpans, glass casseroles with a cover, pie tins with plastic covers, aluminum cake pans with plastic covers | Flats and trays for starting seeds and rooting cuttings |
| Milk cartons | Starting seeds, rooting cuttings, and as a temporary pot |
| All cans with a plastic cover to replace the original one—coffee cans, mixed nut cans, Crisco cans | Containers in which to grow seeds |

| Toothpicks | Support for growing pits, tubers, and yams |
| --- | --- |
| Cat litter (unused!) | To replace vermiculite and perlite as soil lighteners |
| Charcoal | Added to soil and water to promote healthy growth |
| Transparent, plastic shower cap | Place over seed-growing container to make miniature greenhouse — support plastic with label sticks or tongue depressors |
| Plastic prize containers given to children in restaurants | Ideal for germinating seeds |
| Styrofoam cups | Individual pots for young cuttings |
| Plastic cups | Inverted over newly transplanted cutting for greenhouse effect |
| Clorox | Mixed with water to sterilize pots (nine parts water to one part Clorox) |
| Sieve | For sifting peat or potting soil |
| Spatula | Use to transplant seedlings |

| | |
|---|---|
| Cypress, cedar, and redwood tubs; bottoms of wine barrels | Tubs or pots for large plants and trees |
| Plastic ice cream containers | Pots, specifically a Forsyth pot |
| Plastic dry-cleaner's bags | Tent for raising humidity, strips for air layering |
| Plastic bags (such as Baggies) or packages from frozen corn and peas, plastic sacks for holding potatoes | Holds seeds for "wintering," cut into strips for air layering, small tents to raise humidity, and "pot" for cuttings |
| Plastic wash basket, waste basket, and trash can. | Can be used as tubs or pots for large plants |
| Miniature plastic terrariums | Made by Jay V. Zimmerman Co., 7777 Bonhomme, St. Louis, Missouri 63105 |
| Cheesecloth | Germinating seeds |
| Pencil or tongue depressor | Necessary for transplanting seedlings |
| Large glass gallon jars for juice, vinegar, and cider | Terrariums and when cut off, used as a greenhouse |
| Aquarium | Greenhouse for seeds and cuttings; excellent terrarium |
| Marbles and pebbles | Placed in saucers to raise pot above water level |

| | |
|---|---|
| Heating pad,* heating coils (sold by many florists and seed companies) | Helps raise temperature for germinating seeds |
| Margarine tubs, old soup dishes, large bowls, shallow enamel bins | Saucers for pots |
| Shell No-pest strip | Used in plastic tent to kill bugs |
| Plastic garbage bags | Tent for killing insects; lining under plants "taking a vacation" in a tub |

You probably have many of these items in your house. All of them can help you cut costs in growing plants from scratch. One expense worth bearing is that of soil. Make sure you buy *sterilized* soil. You can also purchase peat moss, vermiculite, perlite, and sphagnum moss (in nurseries and florist shops) as well as numerous brands of fine fertilizer. None of these are extremely expensive. Naturally, it pays to buy in bulk—this is particularly true with soil. You'll need much more than you would think. Get as large a bag as possible. It takes up little space and stores well.

* For information write Northern Electric Company, 5224 North Kedze, Chicago, Illinois 60625.

## THE SECRET TO SUCCESSFUL POTTING

You'll discover that potting seedlings, cuttings, and mature plants is quite easy if you follow these steps:

(1)  If the plant is going to be potted in a clay pot, place several pieces of broken pottery over the bottom drainage hole to prevent soil from leaking out or from packing which prevents drainage. You can also use small pebbles or rocks, but be sure the rocks are clean by sterilizing them in boiling water.

(2)  Water can evaporate through the sides of a clay pot, but this isn't true with a plastic pot. For this reason you need to be very careful in watering a plant in a plastic pot. Make sure the plant will never have wet feet for any long period of time. To prevent this, place a full inch of crocking at the bottom of the plastic pot. This provides more drainage than in a clay pot.

(3)  Pour ¼ inch of pulverized charcoal over the crocking. This is available in many florist shops. This is not an essential step, but it will keep the soil from going sour.

(4)  When filling the pot with soil and the plant, make sure there is enough space for watering. Tap the pot on a hard surface to fill in any air pockets in the soil.

(5)  Place the plant directly in the center of the pot. You may have to add more soil or take some away so that the plant is in the correct position—neither resting too low nor too high in the pot.

(6)  The ideal position is one which allows for easy watering. In a large pot (10 inches) the plant should be 1 inch

**1**

**2**

Clay pots breathe and need to be watered more frequently than plastic pots. A single piece of crocking over the drainage hole will prevent soil from packing or running out when watered.

Plastic pots retain water and do not need the frequent watering of clay pots. Most plastic pots have several small drainage holes in the bottom. You should put more crocking into plastic pots for perfect drainage.

**3 & 4**

It's easy to root many cuttings in water as a way of starting plants from scratch. When you transfer a plant from water to soil, try not to bury the stem any deeper than it was resting in water.

from the top of the pot. Even in the smallest pot you should leave at least 1/4 inch of space for watering.

(7) Fill in the space between the plant and the pot with soil. Pack the soil firmly by pressing down on it with the side of your thumb. Rotate the pot slowly as the soil is being packed to make sure that the soil is firm all the way around the plant. Add new soil whenever necessary to fill in space left after packing. Finally, the new soil should be on the same level as the old soil around the plant.

(8) Soak the plant thoroughly so that the new soil is firmly in place. If you notice any gaps in the soil, fill them in and water again.

(9) Follow the preceding eight steps when potting cuttings and seedlings. *Never bury the bottom two leaves when transplanting tiny plants.* When you pot a cutting, place the roots deep into the soil. Make sure that the soil is packed firmly around seedlings and cuttings, otherwise they will topple over when watered.


### Getting plants out of pots

Most plants slip out of their pots with very little trouble if you hold them upside down and give the edge of the pot a good rap on a hard surface. Support the plant between your middle and forefinger. Sometimes, small plants seem to be stuck in the pot. Check the drainage hole to see if roots are sticking out. If they are, push them through the hole toward the top of the pot with the blunt end of a pencil or stick. Running a knife around the edge of the pot often helps to loosen a plant from the pot.

Large, treelike plants can be difficult to get out of a pot. Give them a good soaking a day ahead of time. Run a knife around the inside edge of the pot. Tap the pot several times on its sides as hard as you can. With the help of another person, see whether you can get the plant to slide out by resting it on its side or at an angle while you pull gently on the main root ball around the base of the plant. If it doesn't budge, you should break the pot rather than risk a broken trunk (and back).

## STARTING FROM SCRATCH WITH SEEDS

Each grower has his own formula for success in growing plants from seeds. Following is a brief guide outlining the basic steps in starting from scratch.

(1) Prepare a pot or flat containing a moisture-retaining mixture of soil. Both the pot and flat should have drainage holes. If you use a pot, crock it with drainage material such as small pebbles. Fill it with *sterilized* potting soil leaving just over an inch of space at the top of the pot. Cover the soil with a thin ¼-inch layer of peat or fine-grade vermiculite (some growers prefer to mix them together). If you use a flat, cover the bottom with ½ inch of small pebbles. Charcoal can be sprinkled over the pebbles to keep the soil above fresh. Fill the flat with sterilized soil leaving about 1½ inches of space at the top. Cover the soil with ¼ inch of peat, vermiculite, or a combination of both.

(2) Pack the mixture lightly with a flat object (such as a book) until the surface is even.

**1**

Seeds should be planted in a 3-to-4-inch bed made up of perlite, vermiculite, sterilized soil, or sand. Sometimes a mixture of these is best. Be sure to use containers with holes in the bottom to allow for adequate drainage.

**2**

Mist the growing medium thoroughly before planting seeds. No water should be left standing on the surface of the growing medium.

**3**

Sprinkle the seeds evenly across the surface of the growing medium or in shallow rows. You may have to tap the packet with your finger to get the seeds to sprinkle out evenly.

**4**

Mist the seeds until the entire surface is moist and cover the container with a piece of glass or plastic. Leave a corner of the flat or pan uncovered to allow air to circulate above the seeds.

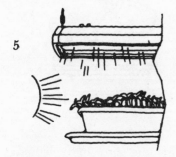

5

Seedlings are responsive to outside light sources. They tend to lean in the direction of the sun. You'll have to turn a flat frequently to encourage uniform growth. However, grow lights placed above the sprouting plants can supplement or take the place of natural light, and the plants will grow straight up toward the light source. Plants directly under the center of artificial light often grow slightly faster than those at the end.

6

As soon as seedlings have a second pair of leaves, pot them in individual pots. Hold the plant between your forefinger and thumb. Grab a leaf rather than a stem, which damages easily. Pot the plant as deeply as possible without burying the bottom leaves.

(3) Mist the soil until it is thoroughly moist. You can also place the pot or flat in a sink or tub to let moisture seep through the drainage holes. When the surface of the soil is moist, take the pot or flat out of the water.

(4) Sow the seeds on the moist surface, spreading them as evenly as possible. With miniscule seeds, tap the packet with your forefinger. If the packet is at just the right angle, the seeds will be sprinkled finely over the entire soil surface.

(5) Cover the seeds with finely pulverized soil. Seeds should be covered to the depth equal to three times their width. Tiny seeds can rest on the surface of the soil without being covered at all.

(6) Mist the seeds and new soil until they are moist.

(7) Cover the flat with plastic or a pane of glass. Some homemade flats (made from plastic bread boxes, aluminum cake pans, and casseroles) already have plastic or glass tops which fit securely over the top. Be sure to lift the top daily for air movement!

(8) Try to keep the temperature high. The range between 75° and 85° is ideal. Plants at the seed stage generally need no light.

(9) Lift the cover daily to make sure that the soil surface is moist. Mist the soil at the slightest hint of dryness. The soil should never be soggy.

(10) As soon as the seeds begin to sprout, move them into either direct or indirect light depending upon the kind of seed you're growing. Instructions about this step are on seed packages. Also, allow some fresh air to circulate around the plants. You can remove the cover completely, but be very careful to mist the plants when the soil begins to dry out. You can also slant the cover at an angle to keep the humidity high.

(11) Once the plants are above the surface of the soil, most will thrive in a temperature of 70° to 72° unless otherwise indicated.

(12) With proper light and watering the plants will grow quickly. If they begin to lean at an angle toward outside light, keep rotating the flat a few degrees each day. You

may have to do this several times unless your source of light is directly above the plants—one of the real advantages of fluorescent lights.

(13) Usually, more plants grow than you can use. Thinning plants allows a few to grow well. Since you don't want to disturb the root system of any plant, don't pull unwanted plants from the soil. Snip them out at soil level with a scissors.

(14) As soon as the plants produce true leaves—the second pair of leaves to appear on the plant—you can transplant them into small 2¼-inch individual pots. Exceptions to this rule are carefully pointed out in other chapters.

(15) Transplanting young seedlings can shock them and should be done very carefully. Several hours before transplanting, water the plants gently so that the soil is moist. Use a tongue depressor, spatula, or similar object to help you scoop the plant from the soil. Try to get as much soil with each plant as possible. Sometimes, all you get is a root. Try to hold the plant by the leaves instead of the stem which is easily damaged. Place the root or tiny ball of earth into a hole poked in the soil of the new pot. Make sure *that the bottom leaves of a seedling are never buried.* Pack the soil around the plant so that it has support. Trickle water into the pot and give the plant a good misting until the soil is thoroughly moist.

(16) Seedlings which have just been transplanted should be given *indirect* light.

(17) For a few days you may want to cover the plant with a plastic bag to keep the humidity high around it. This is often helpful, but not necessary.

(18) As soon as the plant is growing well, you can place it in increasingly brighter light.

(19) Young seedlings often are attacked by a soil-borne fungus which causes "damping off," a condition which results in a seedling's toppling over and dying. By using sterilized soil you can prevent many attacks by this fungus. You can also buy fungicides (Banrot, Truban, or Captan) which will help you avoid cases of damping off in precious plants. Banrot and Truban as a combined treatment is particularly potent.

## HOW TO MAKE CUTTINGS ROOT

Many cuttings taken from plants will root directly in water. English ivy, philodendron, coleus, geranium, and wandering Jew are but a few examples. Cuttings from different plants can be dusted with a rooting hormone and planted in moist sand, vermiculite, perlite, or peat. The process of taking cuttings is described for each plant in preceding chapters, but here are a few overall tips.

(1) When you root cuttings directly in water, place some charcoal at the bottom of the glass or bottle to keep the water fresh. Cuttings grow best in opaque jars.

(2) Cuttings will root in sand, vermiculite, or perlite if kept continually moist. The best rooting medium is indicated for individual plants under their entry.

(3) Most cuttings should be dusted with rooting hormone before being planted in soil. A light covering of the white powder on the end of the cutting is all that is needed.

**1**

**2**

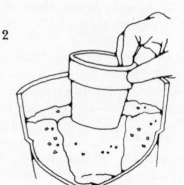

Cover the drainage hole in a 2¼-inch clay pot with strapping tape. You can only do this if the pot is dry. Or plug the hole with cork, clay, or bubble gum.

Place the clay pot in a 6-inch plastic pot filled with perlite, vermiculite, sterile sand, or a combination of the three.

**3**

Keep the small clay pot filled with water so that the surrounding rooting medium will be kept uniformly moist. This is the classic Forsyth pot, an ideal solution for starting cuttings from scratch.

This hormone also contains a fungicide to stop root rot. Inexpensive packets of *Rootone* or *Hormidin* are available in many florist shops and garden supply centers.

(4) *The Forsyth pot*: If you're using a large plastic pot as a growing bed for cuttings, place a small clay pot in the center. Plug the hole in the bottom of the smaller clay pot with a piece of cork or cover it with strapping tape. Keep the smaller pot filled with water, which will seep slowly into the surrounding vermiculite or sand of the plastic pot, thereby keeping it moist.

(5) Cuttings planted in a pot can be kept moist by covering the entire pot with half of a large glass bottle or jar. Slide small wooden blocks under the edge of the jar to allow air inside.

(6) Cuttings planted in a pot can be kept moist by covering the pot with a plastic bag—a good reason to save the bags from the dry cleaners. The bag should not be allowed to touch the leaves. Use bent coat hangers or sticks to prop the bag up. The plastic can be sealed at the bottom of the pot with a large rubber band. If water begins to collect on the inside of the bag, open it for a short time to let some fresh air in. If the inside of the bag is continually cloudy, punch a few holes in the top. The atmosphere around a cutting should be humid, but not muggy.

(7) If you're planting a number of cuttings in a flat, cover the flat with polyethylene to raise the humidity. Bent clothes hangers or croquet wickets make ideal props to keep the plastic from touching plants underneath.

(8) Single cuttings can be kept moist by inverting a jar over the top of the plant.

(9) Single or several cuttings can be placed in plastic bags with enough growing medium for them to root.

(10) Aquariums make excellent miniature greenhouses, nearly duplicating the ideal growing conditions of a hot-house.

(11) Some cuttings rot in a humid environment. Plants such as begonias, geraniums, kalanchoes, and peperomia prefer an airy and open place in which to grow. Don't cover them.

(12) Check the growing medium frequently when trying to get cuttings to root. If the sand or vermiculite is allowed to dry out, the plants will probably die.

(13) Unlike seeds, cuttings need good light in which to grow.

## WHEN TO WATER AND WHEN *NOT* TO

Plants, like people, have completely different needs and habits. These needs are clearly indicated in each chapter. However, certain general rules apply to all plants.

(1) Saturate a plant when you water it. Don't be timid. If there is proper drainage in the pot, then any excess water will run out from the hole in the bottom. You've watered the plant properly when water trickles through this hole. No water should be standing on the surface of the soil within several minutes of watering.

(2) Only water when necessary. *You can't tell when to water by looking at the soil.* Use your fingers to tell

whether it's drying out or not. Stick your finger an inch into the soil. Moist soil sticks to the end of your finger. Most plants thrive in moist soil, but they don't like wet feet. Soggy soil is deadly over any length of time. The loss of indoor plants is often caused by overwatering—a common error. Only water the plant when the soil is dry below the surface.

(3) The soil in clay pots dries out much faster than that in plastic pots. Clay pots breath and lose water quickly through evaporation.

(4) Experienced gardeners prefer to water plants in the morning. This gives soil a chance to get rid of any excess moisture in the heat of the day. This is one rule which many people disregard, fortunately without any serious damage to plants.

(5) If you have fluoridated water, consider using distilled water on plants that can not tolerate fluoride (ti, spider, and prayer plants). Unfortunately, distilled water must be purchased.

(6) If you mix too much peat with potting soil, the water tends to stand on the surface without being absorbed. Peat is an excellent way to make soil light and airy, but don't go overboard, or you'll have a hard time watering your plants effectively.

(7) Germinating seeds should be watered with a mister in order not to disturb the tiny root systems.

(8) When growing cuttings in water, add some charcoal to the glass. This helps the water stay fresh.

(9) *Water all your plants with tepid water.* Plants adore warm water and respond lovingly. Any plants with fuzzy leaves such as African violets require warm water.

(10) Mist plants only when out of direct sunlight. Otherwise, the foliage will get spotted with burns. Mist the plant in shade, allow the foliage to dry, and then return the plant to bright light.

## HOW TO OVERCOME THE CONDITIONS OF A DRY APARTMENT

The lack of humidity in modern apartments and houses is the main cause of "brown" and "black" thumbs. Naturally, a central humidifier is an obvious solution. Even if you don't have one, here are some simple ways to provide moisture for those humidity-loving indoor plants.

(1) All plants should be potted in such a way that water can drain from the opening in the bottom of the pot. To increase the humidity around a plant let this water collect in a dish filled with pebbles or marbles directly under the pot. You can fill this dish at any time when the water level seems low. Several plants can be placed in one large dish or pan as well. Never let the water level reach the bottom of the pot where the roots might get wet.

(2) You can also increase the humidity around a plant by double potting. Place a potted plant in a larger pot with pebbles or marbles at the bottom. Fill in the space between the sides of the pot with sphagnum moss. Soak the moss with water. This will raise the relative humidity around the plant.

(3) Humidity is higher around groups of plants. Grouping your plants also makes watering less of a chore.

(4) Most plants like to be misted frequently. A fine spray of water should be applied to both the top and bottom of the leaves. Misting raises the humidity and also effectively destroys many plant pests.

(5) To give your plants a special treat, let them take a shower with you. Bring them into the bathroom where they can breathe the warm humid air.

(6) Wash plants frequently with tepid water by dunking the foliage into a sink or tub. Soot and grime will slowly kill plants unless it is removed. Most plants adore warm baths.

(7) Any plant with thick fleshy leaves would benefit by being sponged with warm water. A sponge bath of the upper sides of the leaves is ideal. Be sure to support the leaf with your hand as you bathe it. Large plants which are hard to move are the most likely candidates for a sponge bath.

## BASIC TIPS ON TEMPERATURE

Before the turn of the century many plants thrived in the cool humid apartments that were prevalent in that era. During the Victorian period, ferns were especially fashionable and grew beautifully under these environmental conditions. With central heating, apartments have become quite dry, less humid, and very warm so that it's now possible to grow a wider range of plants including ones more appropriate for a jungle. Therefore, controlling the temperature is no longer the problem it once was decades ago. Ideal growing temperatures for each plant have been noted throughout the book. You'll probably want to grow plants suited to the temperature you prefer. Avid indoor gardeners trying to grow exotic plants may be forced to raise temperatures above the comfort level in winter. Here are a few overall tips on temperature:

(1) Germinating seeds like high temperatures. You may want to supply bottom heat with special cables, heating pads, or radiators. You can buy small greenhouses from many seed companies. The miniature growing units are about 1½ feet wide and 2 feet long. Make sure they have heating wires or coils in the bottom.

(2) The majority of plants need lower evening temperatures than day. A drop of 10° is ideal. This allows the plants to use food manufactured in the day.

(3) Glass placed over a flat with seedlings can magnify the sun's rays and scorch young leaves. Therefore, be careful.

(4) Although plants enjoy fresh air, they react badly to drafts. A cold draft can kill some tropical plants and will hurt most indoor plants. During cold spells open windows after plants have been removed from that area. During the winter keep plants away from cold window panes, outside doorways, and heating ducts.

## TEN BASIC RULES ON LIGHT

The amount and type of light best suited to individual plants has been carefully outlined in the section on each plant. In summary, here are a few of the most important considerations to keep in mind:

(1) Start plants which will grow well in the light available in your apartment or house.

(2) If your apartment is without natural light, you can grow many plants under fluorescent lights.

(3) Fluorescent lights should never be left on for more than 18 hours a day, since all plants need rest.

(4) Plants with thick fleshy leaves generally need less light than other plants. Cacti and succulents are obvious exceptions.

(5) Bright foliage plants will retain their color only if given plenty of light. Coleus and croton plants need lots of sunshine to make their leaves vibrant.

(6) The amount of light naturally varies with each season. A northern exposure in the summer is the equivalent of an eastern or western exposure in the winter.

(7) Northern exposure, the favorite among artists, has the least light throughout the year while the southern exposure has the most. Both east and west offer good indirect light. A hand passing in front of a plant should cast a shadow in full east or west exposures.

(8) Most germinating seeds need no light at all.

(9) When a seedling begins to emerge through the soil, move it *gradually* into increasingly brighter light. Do the same for mature plants as they can go into shock if moved from a shady area directly into a southern exposure.

(10) Both seedlings and mature plants bend toward the source of light. Move the flat or pot several degrees each

**1**

Since plants reach for outside light, you should turn pots each day to encourage uniform growth.

**2**

Move plants gradually from low light areas to bright ones. Plants accustomed to a shady corner may react badly to direct light in a southern window, so move a plant in steps.

**3**

When you pot or transplant a plant, don't put it in direct light until it's had a chance to take root. Bright light can damage a newly potted plant. Shift the plant slowly from indirect light to bright light.

**4**

Outside light can be affected by curtains, shades, and obstacles such as trees. A southern exposure with a tree shading a plant is really more like an eastern or western exposure.

day to keep the plants looking full and evenly distributed within the pot.

## RULES OF THUMB FOR FERTILIZING

Common sense and experience will soon show you the needs of particular house plants, whether it's your favorite philodendron or spiky pineapple.

(1) Follow the directions on most packages of fertilizer. Sometimes, you may want to cut the recommended dosage by a half. Certain plants require weak dosages of fertilizer as indicated throughout the book.

(2) Scrape off surface soil and remove old soil around the edge of the pot every few months. Replace with fresh soil. This is a natural way to give the plant added nutrients.

(3) Vary a plant's diet to see which fertilizer appeals to it most. Both organic and inorganic fertilizers are readily available in most retail florist shops.

(4) Don't fertilize a plant which has just been potted or transplanted. Wait at least 3 months.

(5) Never fertilize a sick plant unless you think the cause of disease is a lack of food. You can repot the plant adding fresh soil to see whether this is really the case.

(6) Fertilize once a month in the spring and summer when a plant is growing rapidly. Fertilize every 6 to 8 weeks during the late fall and winter.

(7) When you move a plant from one area to another, don't fertilize until it gets accustomed to its new spot.

(8) Slow-release fertilizers are now available on the market. They are probably the safest way to fertilize plants. Follow the directions on the label.

## HOW TO IDENTIFY AND AVOID PLANT PESTS

Insects can be troublesome and harm indoor plants. So you'll want to take appropriate steps to make sure that your plants remain insect-free.

(1) Use only sterilized pots. New clay and plastic pots are sterile. However, each time you reuse a pot, you should clean it thoroughly. Scrub clay pots inside and out with a heavy wire brush under hot running water. Wash the pot in a solution of nine parts water to one part chlorine bleach. Rinse the pot with clear water to wash off traces of the bleach. If you have no chlorine bleach, pour boiling water over the clean pot. Plastic pots should be scrubbed clean, rinsed with hot water, and allowed to dry.

(2) Use sterilized soil for all potting and transplanting. This is available in most florist shops. The cost of sterilized soil is worth the expense. Preparing your own in an apartment would be time consuming and impractical.

(3) By keeping your plants clean you'll avoid most pests. Just turn the plant upside down and swish the foliage in a basin filled with warm water. Plants respond well to this.

(4) Mist plants frequently in the winter to discourage such plant killers as red spider mites. Be sure to mist the undersides of the leaves as well as the tops!

(5) If you ever bring a new plant into your apartment, keep it isolated from your other plants for several weeks. This is the only way you can be sure that it's not infected with some pest or disease. Either should show up in that time.

(6) Isolate any plant that is infested with insects. Your other plants will have a better chance of escaping attack.

(7) Five insects are the most common pests to indoor house plants. If you can learn to recognize them before they do too much damage, you'll have a good chance of saving your plants.

## Five pests to look for and what to do

(1) **Aphids** (plant lice) are tiny insects which can be green, red, black, or gray. They move slowly enough for you to pick them off the plant by hand. Destroy as many as you can before swishing the foliage of the plant in warm soapy water. Afterwards, rinse off the foliage with warm clear water. Large plants can be cleaned with a soapy sponge and rinsed off with a wet cloth.

(2) **Mealybugs** look like clumps of cotton underneath leaves or at the joints of a plant. Destroy this white fuzz by touching it with a Q-tip dipped in alcohol. After dabbing the insects in this way, wash the foliage of the plant in warm soapy water. Afterwards, rinse off the foliage with warm clear water.

(3) **Red spider mites** pose a serious threat to your plants. These miniscule insects spot the undersides of leaves so they look as if they have been sprinkled with paprika. Ultra-fine white webs appear under the leaves. Wash the plant in warm water. If too many leaves are infected, it's best to destroy the plant and discard the soil. This insect is one of the few really deadly pests in indoor gardens.

(4) **Scales** appear as tiny white, gray, or brown bumps or oval spots on the underside of leaves and on the main stem of a plant. These insects mimic natural spots on plants so that they are often hard to notice. However, they do secrete a sticky substance which you can feel with your fingers. Scrub scales off leaves and the main stem of a plant with a toothbrush or sponge dipped in soapy water. Afterwards, rinse them with clear water.

(5) **White flies** hover like miniature moths around a plant while their young slowly eat away the foliage. You may be able to suck up the adult white flies with your vacuum cleaner. To get rid of other adult insects on the plant wash both the bottom and the top of every leaf with warm water. Use the "No-Pest Strip" method outlined below to assure removal. Treat the plants every other day for a week to kill consecutive hatchings.

**If all else fails . . .**

You may have to wash the plants several times before you get rid of these pests. If several attempts fail, either destroy the plant or use an insecticide known as the Shell No-Pest Strip. Follow these steps carefully:

(1) Wear plastic gloves.

(2) Cut the strip into four sections. Enclose three sections in aluminum foil, mark them clearly, and store them out of the reach of children.

(3) Take the fourth section and attach it with a piece of string or wire to the bottom of a clothes hanger.

(4) Poke the curved end of the hanger through the sealed end of a large plastic garbage bag.

(5) Hang the bag in a dark closet.

(6) Place the infected plant through the opening at the bottom of the plastic bag. Use a piece of sturdy cardboard to support the pot. Seal the bag underneath the pot so that the plant is in a "vacuum" with the No-Pest Strip.

(7) Leave the plant in the bag for 8 to 12 hours. Remove the plant from the bag after this time and place it out of direct sunlight for a day. If you've never used this method on a plant before, check every 2 hours to see if the plant looks healthy. If it's beginning to wilt, take it out of the bag. If it looks fine, leave it in for the full treatment. You have to repeat this treatment every other day for a week to get rid of scale, mealybugs, red spider mites, or white flies. This week-long treatment generally destroys these pests, but you may have to put the plant through a second and even a third treatment if the bugs come back. One 8- to 12-hour treatment usually takes care of aphids.

Leaving a plant in a bag with the No-Pest Strip for over 12 hours can be dangerous to its health. Research scientists have recently discovered that this prolonged treatment can cause genetic reactions in plants resulting in either unusually poor or spectacularly new-colored varieties. Never use this treatment on begonias!

## TAKING A VACATION?

Assuming that you can't find a plant sitter to water your plants from time to time, here are some ideas on how to keep your plants alive while you're gone.

(1) If you only have one plant, give it a good soaking until water collects in the dish below. Drain the excess water from the dish. Cover the entire plant and dish with a large plastic bag. Make sure that the plastic isn't touching the leaves. Sticks, clothes hangers, and some kitchen utensils can all be used as makeshift "tent poles." Keep the plant in a sink or tub out of direct sunlight.

(2) If you have several plants, you can group them together and cover them with an even larger plastic bag in the same way. Bags from the dry cleaner work well. As long as the plants have been well watered, they should survive for 3 weeks in this flimsy terrarium. Keep the plants out of direct sunlight. Perhaps you'll want to put them in a tub (as follows).

(3) If you have many plants, line your tub with several layers of newspaper placed on top of a plastic bag (such as one from the cleaners). Turn on the shower until all of the paper is wet. Cover the paper with another plastic bag and turn on the shower again just long enough to get the plastic moist. Place the plants on the plastic after giving them a good soaking. Cover all the plants with several large plastic bags using masking tape to hold the bags in place. Poke a few small holes in the plastic covering for some fresh air. If there's a window in the bathroom, don't pull the shade. Otherwise, turn on a light and let it stay on while you're gone. This is not treating your plants the way they'd like to be, but they should survive.

(4) Huge humidity-loving plants can also be covered with a large plastic bag which can be tied to the main stem just below the leaves. Soak the soil thoroughly.

(5) When using any of these methods to reduce water loss from the plant, be sure to remove any dead leaves from the plant, remove all flowers, and pinch off all flower buds.

No hobby has brought so much joy to so many millions of people as starting plants from scratch. Creating a fern from a spore, a bushy deep-green mango tree from a large seed, or a brightly flowering geranium from a fleshy stem—each will bring you closer to both the mystery and miracle of nature.

The green touch is a unique blend of patience, love, and skill. Anyone can learn to have it. With over 350,000 plants in the world, you have an infinite variety to discover and enjoy.

**JOHN WHITMAN** studied at Princeton University and the University of Minnesota. He was a grower at Bachman's, the largest retail florist and nursery in the United States.


**MARY MAGUIRE** has a B.S. in horticulture and is the Education Officer at the Como Park Conservatory in St. Paul, Minnesota. A specialist in floriculture, she is a regular columnist for the *Minneapolis Tribune*.